# partyhawaiʻi

# partyhawai'i

## A GUIDE TO **ENTERTAINING** IN THE ISLANDS

kaui philpotts

PHOTOGRAPHY BY
*kaz tanabe + david franzen*

MUTUAL PUBLISHING

Library of Congress Cataloging-in-Publication Data

Philpotts, Kaui.
Party Hawai'i : a guide to entertaining in the islands / Kaui Philpotts ; photography by Kaz Tanabe + David Franzen.
p. cm.
ISBN-13: 978-1-56647-840-3
ISBN-10: 1-56647-840-5 (hardcover : alk. paper)
1. Hawaiian cookery. 2. Luaus. 3. Entertaining. I. Title. II. Title: Party Hawaii.
TX724.5.H3P456 2007
641.59969--dc22
2007029476

First Printing, October 2007
1 2 3 4 5 6 7 8 9

ISBN-10: 1-56647-840-5
ISBN-13: 978-1-56647-840-3

Book design by Julie Chun Design
Photos by David Franzen appear on the following pages:
vi (center), 7, 8 (top), 42-43, 44, 46-49, 51, 60-61, 62, 64, 65, 68, 69, 72, 94-95, 96, 98, 100, 101, 105, 109, 111, 195
All other photos by Kaz Tanabe

**MUTUAL PUBLISHING, LLC**
1215 Center Street, Suite 210
Honolulu, Hawai'i 96816
Ph: (808) 732-1709
Fax: (808) 734-4094
Email: info@mutualpublishing.com
www.mutualpublishing.com

Printed in China

# contents

# FOREWORD

*"The best host is not he who spends the most money to entertain his guests, but he who takes the most intelligent interest in their welfare and makes sure that they will have a good time, something good to drink, something that is both good and new, if possible."*

—Andre Simon in *Never Eat More Than You Can Lift*
by Sharon Tyler Herbst

Entertaining is an act that can be as simple as having a neighbor over for a cup of coffee or as complex as throwing a wedding party for hundreds. It's a gesture of hospitality, a way to bring people together to share a moment in time, and its measure of success is if everyone feels comfortable and has a good time.

In Hawai'i, entertaining can run the gamut of a beach park barbecue, a carport cookout, an afternoon tea, a poi supper, brunch at a dim sum restaurant, tailgating at a sports event, a sit-down dinner by the pool, or a candlelight dinner for two. It's about the place, the ambiance, the food, and the people. Each element of entertaining is an expression of the host's personality and what he or she wants to share with family, business associates, neighbors, and friends.

As someone who loves to entertain, I'm always observing how others do it. Few people do it with warmth and exuberance like Kaui Philpotts. Born and raised on the Islands, an author and newspaper columnist for many years, Kaui entertains with the personal flair and comfortable hospitality we all strive for. She's known for elevating simple gatherings to fabulous affairs, planning and paying attention to

the many details for a successful party.

What's great about Kaui is that she's practical, too. Entertaining in style doesn't have to be complicated: it can be as simple as taking prepared food out of their store-bought containers and putting it into a pretty bowl from your kitchen cupboard. It doesn't have to be expensive: it can mean searching for table décor at a "big box" discount store or simply cutting flowers and greenery from your backyard. Nor does entertaining mean you have to do it all yourself: caterers and restaurants can provide the essential elements while you concentrate on the rest of the details.

For many people, entertaining is a daunting task. But it need not be. Let *Party Hawai'i* serve as a guide for some wonderful, stylish, and no doubt memorable get-togethers that you can accomplish with a little planning and organizing. Let this book be also a starting point for more ideas of your own in order to create those memorable moments that you share with others.

*Joan Namkoong*

FOOD JOURNALIST AND
FARMER'S MARKET ORGANIZER

# INTRODUCTION

When you get right down to it, Island people love laughing, feeling celebrated, and connecting with others. There is something special about knowing that someone has put in a lot of thought and effort to show you a good time.

Since the discovery of Hawai'i by the British in the late eighteenth century, Hawaiians have been known for their hospitality and welcoming nature. (Well, okay, maybe Captain Cook didn't fare too well.) When Western ways took hold, it wasn't long before they blended the old with the new into a potpourri of party styles.

Add in the exotic cultures introduced from Asia, each with their own set of holidays and celebrations, and the mix becomes particularly delicious. Living in the Islands has always meant living with this special blend and celebrating each other's festivals— bon dances, lantern send-offs, malassadas on Fat Tuesdays, Lei Day, and the making of gau at Chinese New Year.

Contemporary Hawai'i is spiritually connected to both the mainland U.S. and Asia by the influx of goods and people brought by a robust visitor industry, and the result is like no place else on earth. This book embraces the similarities and differences of Hawai'i's diverse cultures.

*Party Hawai'i* is a "how-to" book that focuses on the way we entertain today, whether it's a luncheon on the grounds of Queen Emma's summer palace, or a dinner party at an 85-year-old Japanese teahouse high above the city. We show you how to shop in Chinatown the way locals do and introduce you to party themes you may never have considered. It shows how much like everyone else we are—and how different with our baby lū'au, sunset weddings on the beach, and mochi pounding at the New Year.

Island people are not on vacation. They are as work-obsessed, stressed and busy as anyone anywhere. More often than not, they entertain with food that is either prepared by a restaurant or market, catered, or assembled by many, such as a potluck. What they serve is as varied as potato salad with Korean BBQ ribs and haupia squares.

While working on this book I was taken by how "mainstream" Hawai'i has become in just the last twenty years. Today's parties are more sophisticated and yet relaxed at the same time. The host may be serving lychee martinis, but all the shoes are off in a tumble at the front door. Island parties are, more often than not, multigenerational, a team effort, with different people contributing different parts. We have big 'ohana and we love getting together. We love giving lei and favors at events.

This book is meant to stimulate ideas in anyone who loves to have guests over but finds it daunting. It is about personal entertaining, not the sort done for fundraising events or business. Hopefully it gives the meek the courage to invite friends over, to mix it up, and relax while they're doing it.

When you turn the last page, pick up the phone or send an email—and *Party Hawai'i!*

*Kaui Philpotts*

# THE BASICS

# THE BASICS

Your best friend's getting married, you scored a great beach house for the weekend, or the weather has been perfectly gorgeous—whatever the reason, you think it's time to throw a party.

Before you spin yourself into overwhelm, step back and look at the basics. If you're a nervous party-giver, enlist a friend or relative and start to plan. This book will give you tried-and-true ways to get you started.

Planning is the key to any event that stands out.
Don't be afraid to get help from pros, delegate tasks to friends and family, or be crazy and creative. In the end, if everything isn't perfect, forget it and have a good time. Chances are your party is already much better than you know.

Thinking a party through ahead of time and paying attention to the little details are what make it special. Your favorite foods, flowers, and pastimes are all great places to begin designing a great event. Just remember that being too rigid about the outcome will kill a good time for you and everyone else.

So let's get started on the basics.

## Making a Plan

First, consider why you're having the party. Next, look around at what you've already got on hand. Is there a budget? Are you celebrating a special occasion? Is it a baby's

first birthday or the last chance at a summer bash before Labor Day? What kind of setting is available to you? Are you working with a tiny city apartment or hundreds of acres on a country hillside? All these things will determine what you finally do. So many parties come to mind after you are introduced to a lovely or quirky space, followed by a, "Hey! Wouldn't it be great to have a party here?"

## Place/Setting/Time

So often the place you live inspires the sort of parties you throw. How often have you heard people refer to a particular home as a "great party house?" This goes for weekend places you rent and off-island vacations. The location alone can be the inspiration to throw a party.

You can also let the reason for the party determine the setting. Reasons in Hawai'i are often the same as they are anywhere in the world. However, because Hawai'i's culture is so ethnically diverse, other traditions also come into play. Twenty-first birthdays still signify a coming of age for young people. There are some who throw "Sweet Sixteen" parties for teenage girls—a kind of "coming out." We have Yakudoshi parties for a man's forty-first birthday and baby luau for a child's first.

Many parties are much simpler. Potluck is an Island staple. Super Bowl parties have become very important, as has Halloween, when revelers take to the streets in resort towns like Waikīkī and Lahaina. Marion Philpotts Miller, who lives a non-stop life juggling career and family, chose to throw her own birthday party for 20 friends at a teahouse where the ambience and food were a no-brainer. Being a designer, she just personalized the décor. Most restaurants have private dining rooms and a themed décor already there.

Jeff Finney and Jonathan Staub decided on a weekend on an 'ewa beach which allowed them to celebrate the good weather and gorgeous sunsets. Even if you live in a miniscule studio apartment you can throw a party. You might not have access to beachfront property, but public parks are frequently used in Hawai'i. The wonderful weather makes the day enjoyable for everyone and on any Saturday or Sunday you can see bouncy play houses for children's parties dotting the lawns.

Drive through a neighborhood in the country as I did in Waimanalo one weekend and the smell of food grilling is everywhere. Picnic tables are set up in carports, beer is iced in coolers and children are playing on the grass while someone picks on an 'ukulele. Who says a party can't be as simple as just you and the neighbors?

Match the time you select for your party to the purpose and those attending. Is it being held at the office? A work day, either during the lunch hour or pau hana, is your best choice. Are you inviting several generations where driving is an issue for older people? Consider brunch, lunch, or an early start time.

When the occasion such as a birthday or anniversary is tied to a particular date, it's usually fine to move it to the weekend. Remember you don't need a mob to party. What about a romantic dinner for two at home, or packed up and taken to a favorite spot?

- Determine how many people you can fit comfortably at your dining table, in your living room, or in your apartment. Remember that if a dinner party is more than 6 to 8 people, it's no longer "intimate."

- Cocktail parties in your home are often a way to entertain all the people you like, but never seem to find the time to entertain. So what? You're doing it now. Even if you find these parties superficial—again, so what? They're not meant to be more.

- If money isn't an issue, or if you have access (meaning you know someone important), to a fabulous place, you're halfway there. Just remember you can also have a wonderful party as easily in a garage or the back room of a Chinese restaurant.

- The space you have to work with will determine how many people you can invite. Most parties are more fun with slightly more people than the place can actually hold comfortably. Tight spaces force people to talk to each other and mingle, and you will always have no-shows— so never fear.

- Look for unusual places. A group of young friends recently asked the chef of a Chinatown hole-in-the-wall with fabulous food to open on a night they were normally closed and cook for a group of sixteen friends. There was barely enough room for them all, but they brought in their own tablecloths, candles, wine, and even plates (this place serves on Styrofoam!). The chef contributed the unique, delicious dishes, and a great, if raucous, time was had by all.

## Selecting a Theme

A theme, no matter how wacky, is a good place to start. It can be as simple as picking a favorite color as the "pink party" for Girls' Day or celebrating one's ethnic heritage like the Bollywood Birthday.

A theme helps you determine everything from the invitations, food, and drinks to setting, décor, and favors. It can be as off-the-wall as the Liliko'i Festival, a party a young woman created for her friends simply because the fruit ripening all over the yard delighted her. She served liliko'i (passion fruit) drinks, sauces for grilling, and desserts. Her table centerpieces were bowls filled with the fragrant, yellow fruit.

## Invitations

There's no doubt about it, sending a written invitation heightens the expectations of your party. The invitations should be in the mail at least two weeks prior to the event. For a fancy or holiday season party, make it at least a month. If it's a big event and guests are coming from elsewhere you might want to send a Save the Date card.

Invitations can come in all forms. For a last minute dinner (say you were given a huge fresh salmon by a fisherman back from Alaska), a simple phone call will do.

E-mails have become widely accepted, especially among young party-givers, who have fun creating amusing ones online complete with background and music.

Graceful, more traditional invitations can come on personalized stationery or note cards a week or two prior. Think Jackie Kennedy Onassis.

We are all more likely to buy ready made, fill-in-the blank ones available in stylish stationery shops. These have taken a giant leap forward with the wide use of personal computers. There are any number of fonts available for personalizing your invitations. Take it one step further and create all the paper goods for your party online as was done with the office baby shower. Invitations, place cards and even menus can be produced with ease.

The RSVP number or e-mail address goes on the lower left of the invitation. All the other essentials such as the dress request and parking instructions go on the right. If you need to give a caterer or restaurant a head count, ask for an answer a few days before. People are notoriously bad about RSVPs and will often need to be called. Rude as it is, it's very common.

## Décor and Favors

Let your theme and the setting determine your décor. If you rent a beach house on the North Shore, or find yourself upgraded into a suite on a neighbor Island, your décor is pretty much taken care of for you. The occasion will also determine the décor. For instance, a person's favorite color for a luncheon or wedding shower, or the good luck color red at Chinese New Year or a Yakudoshi.

Beyond that, you need to clear your surfaces. Get rid of magazines, knickknacks and anything that breaks easily. You will need them for food, pūpū, and drinks. Set up extra folding tables if you need them for the bar and buffet. This clean up includes your bathroom counters of personal items and stashing anything you don't want seen (and probably discussed) in your medicine cabinet. Yes, there are people who can't resist looking.

Place fresh flowers and towels in the bathroom. Pretty paper guest hand towels and a nearby wastebasket are nice. Even when you are throwing a large party at a rented location, make sure not to ignore the bathrooms when you prepare.

It's nice if your place can be spotless, but frankly I don't worry too much about that unless the place is already

water, which can also be used in the drinks, and a fruit juice such as orange, grapefruit, or cranberry. Make sure you have something equally nice for non-drinkers. Try creative flavored lemonades or iced tea.

- These days it's fine to offer a selection of good, moderately-priced red and white wines (cabernet sauvignon, merlot, chardonnay, and sauvignon blanc work better than sweeter wines for most people), a premium light beer, and a signature cocktail that relates to your theme or the season. For example, a cool, icy drink like a raspberry-hued Cosmopolitan or Mango Margarita is heaven on warm nights.

- Allow three glasses per guest, and if it's a larger party lasting about two hours, consider renting glasses from a local party-supply house. Hawai'i is a casual, plastic-cup sort of place, but let's face it, if you want to do it right, use real glasses. Remember, it's all about the small things. The exception is when you are entertaining at the pool or beach.

- Have a small chopping board and knife handy, or pre-cut lemons and limes for garnishes. If you're setting up a full bar, make sure to include olives for martinis.

- And speaking of martinis, they've come a long way from a little shaken gin and vermouth. Setting up a martini bar requires a designated bartender, stemmed martini glasses (rented or purchased inexpensively), and a menu of new-style martinis (type it up on your computer, print it out, and frame it for the bar). Taking a little time to set up a martini bar can really make an event sizzle.

# Classics Plus

## negroni

MAKES 1 DRINK

1 ounce gin
1 ounce Campari
1 ounce sweet vermouth

1. Pour ingredients into a cocktail shaker filled with ice.
2. Shake and strain into a cocktail tumbler.
3. Garnish with an orange peel twist.

## pineapple martini

MAKES 6 TO 8 DRINKS

2 cups pineapple juice
2-1/2 cups vodka
1/4 cup vermouth
2 teaspoons Chambord
pineapple chunks and mint to garnish

1. Pour ingredients into a cocktail shaker filled with ice.
2. Shake and strain into a chilled martini glass.
3. Garnish with a skewered pineapple chunk and sprig of mint.

## vodka gimlet

MAKES 1 DRINK

2 ounces vodka
2 tablespoons Rose's lime juice
lime wedge for garnish

1. Pour ingredients into a shaker with ice. Strain into a martini or an old-fashioned glass.
2. Garnish with a wedge of lime.

## margarita

MAKES 1 DRINK

1-1/2 ounces tequila
3/4 ounce triple sec*
1-1/2 tablespoons fresh lime juice
1/2 tablespoon simple syrup
salt

1. Shake ingredients with ice and strain into an old-fashioned glass.
2. To make a salt rim, rub the rim of the glass with lime juice and invert onto a plate of salt.
3. Garnish with lime slices.

✦ *Cointreau or Grand Marnier can be substituted for the triple sec.*

# Classics Plus

## classic martini

MAKES 1 DRINK

2-1/2 ounces gin
1/2 ounce extra dry vermouth, plus a little more
green olive or lemon twist for garnish

1. Rinse the martini glass with a little of the vermouth.
2. Place the gin and vermouth in a shaker filled with ice. Stir and strain into a chilled martini glass.
3. Garnish with a green olive or a lemon twist.

## halekulani's mai tai

MAKES 1 DRINK

1-1/4 ounces mai tai mix
(equal parts of oregeat syrup, orange curacao, and simple syrup)
3/4 ounce amber rum
3/4 ounce black rum
5 ounces fresh lime juice
1/2 ounce dark 151-proof rum
pineapple spear for garnish

1. Pack a glass tumbler with crushed ice.
2. Pour in the mai tai mix, rums, and lime juice.
3. Float the dark rum on top and garnish with an orchid and/or pineapple spear.

## li hing mui cocktail

MAKES 1 DRINK

*This drink is also called a Side Mui and is served at the popular Side Street Inn.*
lime juice

2 ounces sweet & sour
1 ounce vodka
pinch of li hing mui powder
3/4 ounce Kahlúa

1. Prepare a martini glass by running lime juice or water around the rim of the glass.
2. Dip the rim into a plate covered with a tablespoon or so of li hing mui powder.
3. In a shaker, mix the sweet sour mix, vodka, pinch of li hing mui powder, and kahlúa with ice and shake.
4. Pour into the prepared glass.

## mojito

MAKES 4 DRINKS

1/3 cup sugar
1/2 cup fresh mint, roughly chopped
1/2 cup fresh lime juice
1 cup white rum
club soda
lime slices and mint for garnish

1. Place the sugar, fresh mint, and lime juice at the bottom of a small pitcher.
2. With a wooden spoon, muddle or smash the leaves and juice together.
3. Pour in 1 cup white rum.
4. Mix and strain into four 10-ounce glasses filled with crushed ice.
5. Top with club soda.
6. Garnish with lime slices and mint sprigs.

- You can never have too much ice. Stock bags of ice in coolers under the bar or hidden nearby, put some ice in a bucket on the bar, and chill the beer and white wine about two hours prior to the event. Figure two pounds of ice per person. Remember that once beer and wine have been iced, they should remain chilled until consumed. Don't return them to the shelf or storage. Another big don't is putting a bottle of wine in the freezer. You can cool it faster by adding water to the ice in a cooler or ice bucket.

- You will find basic and specialty drink recipes throughout this book.

## Food

Whether you cook the food yourself, order out, or some combination of the two, let the season, your theme, and your serving style determine the menu. In other words, if your guests are balancing plates on their laps all over your living room, don't give them goopy food that needs a knife. Save the fancier, saucier food for small dinner parties, or at least parties where everyone has a place at a table. Buffets are definitely easiest, but will always require more food than sit-down dinners where the portions are controlled.

- One popular caterer likes to always have something interactive happening with the food—such as food being grilled or a sushi chef. It adds to the festive feeling and gives people who may not know each other a chance to "break the ice."

- Plan only the part of the party you love and are good at, and forget about trying to do it all. If you hate to cook and décor is your thing, always be on the alert for great take-out or caterers to do the food.

# THE POI SUPPER

The traditional poi supper is rare today. Once reserved for out-of-town guests or to celebrate anniversaries and birthdays in high style, the poi supper was different than a pāʻina or lūʻau. Think of a lūʻau kicked up a notch or two.

A poi supper consisted of popular Hawaiian dishes: laulau, lomi salmon, poi, kalua pig, chicken or squid lūʻau served with sides of Hawaiian salt, stalks of green onion, and raw round onion. When poi suppers were served buffet style you might also get dishes such as sweet potato with guava jelly glaze or a casserole of lūʻau, crab or chicken, and coconut milk with baked bananas. Desserts were usually fresh coconut cake, pineapple upside-down cake, haupia, and kūlolo. Wine may have been served, but more likely than not, there was a bottle of very good whisky on the table.

Another by-gone feature of poi suppers is the dressy table settings. Coconut bowls, wooden plates, and ti leaves graced the tables which were also complemented with silver, finger bowls, and crystal glasses.

The heyday of the poi supper was in the 20s, 30s, and 40s. However, its popularity lasted well into the 1960s. It's a remnant of a slower, more graceful way of living that is due for a comeback. If you are ever-so-fortunate to be invited to one, drop everything to be there. You won't be sorry.

- Desserts are especially simple to make more tempting by the way they are presented. Dress a store-bought cake with edible fresh flowers, or turn a frozen pound cake into a summer delight with fresh berries and whipped cream. When in a jam, never be ashamed of using cake or brownie mix. Keep it simple. Prepare as much as you can ahead of time.

- Pūpū never needs to be elaborate. Pick up dim sum, poke, or sashimi on your way home. Open a can of salty nuts and pair it with a few wedges of good cheese and crackers. Make store-bought hummus or salsa taste homemade with a squirt of lemon juice and some fresh herbs. People love picking at pūpū.

- The biggest mistake people make is not taking take-out food out of the containers. Sorry, shiny aluminum trays just don't make it! It's so simple—not to mention amazing—how much better food looks placed on serving platters (start collecting inexpensive serving dishes, or fish out your mother's), and garnished with something that's in the dish, such as sliced lemon with lemon chicken or basil leaves with pesto sauce. Parsley is not the only choice. Ti leaves are indispensable on serving trays.

- Match your food to your overall theme. Are you out in the backyard? A barbecue would be natural. Is a friend on their way to Florence? Try a Tuscan menu. You get the idea.

- If you love to cook and have the time, by all means, do so. It doesn't mean you have to make every dish from scratch; plan to start a day or two ahead with things that can be refrigerated (clean out that refrigerator beforehand), and supplement with store-bought items. I have a friend who obsessed so much over the food that she missed her own party by slaving in the kitchen all night. Don't make that mistake.

## Getting Help

- Let your guests help with bartending, pouring water, and simple last-minute preparation. Most people are willing, and it helps them relax. Just don't take it too far. They are there to have a good time. Unless you are entertaining only your closest and dearest family, when you have over fifteen people, get help!

- If you're on a tight budget, enlist a friend or neighbor's son or daughter and pay the equivalent of babysitting money. They can pick up dirty napkins and plates, wash empty glasses, pass the pūpū, and place food on the table.

- Ask friends and acquaintances for recommendations on helpers. Often servers who work in restaurants, or for caterers, will moonlight by helping at private parties. Some are so experienced that you will be able to enjoy your own party. I cannot recommend this highly enough. You can expect to pay $18 to $25 an hour beginning a half hour prior to the party through the clean-up afterward. Be sure to add a 15 to 20 percent tip just as you would in a restaurant. It could be the best money you spend.

- A word of advice on parking: if you are having a large party in a neighborhood where it's difficult to park, call a valet service. For a smaller party, let your guests know ahead of time where to find available parking.

## The Table

For many of us, creating a lovely table is the best part of entertaining. Making your table stand out has more to do with inspiration and an eagle eye for the unexpected than it does with having expensive or formal tableware. It's wonderful if you already have purchased, or inherited, top-quality china, silver, and crystal. Don't you dare leave it unused in boxes, waiting for some grand occasion in the future! Start using it now and allow a lovely, worn patina to develop. Scratches only add to their character.

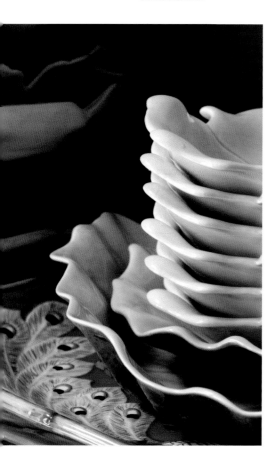  

- If you're beginning with nothing, that's fine, too. Inexpensive sets with classic styling can be found in almost all price ranges. Begin by looking at the tableware in high-end shops, catalogs, and magazines. Rule number one is not to be pretentious. If you can't afford the really good stuff, keep it simple and amusing. The lines should be timeless, clean, and versatile. There are great alternatives in "big box" and discount stores—especially when big-name designers get in the act. For the most part, avoid synthetic fabrics for tableware. Linen and cotton feel, wear, and look so much better.

- A basic white set of dishes is a good place to start. You can add odd pieces of colored or printed plates and bowls. Simple water glasses hold everything from beverages and frozen desserts to flowers and candles. Cut supermarket flower stems short and place them in glasses for a low, tight arrangement. Monochromatic colors work best to complete this look.

- Pillar-style candles don't need special holders. Cluster them on a tray and surround them with pebbles or sand. Anything that works with your theme or colors can go on the table—don't get stuck on just flowers and candles. If you're at the beach, for example, even washed food jars filled with candles, coral, and leaves can serve as table décor.

- Let what's lurking in your closets inspire you. If you like garage sales and secondhand stores, buy bits of mismatched tableware. Odd pairings work when they are tied together by color or theme. One of the most delightful afternoon teas in Honolulu is served on a collection of individually-purchased teacups from yard sales.

- Your serving style will determine how you set up. Family-style meals, where the food is brought to the table in serving dishes and guests serve themselves, works well for casual entertaining. So does buffet-style service when the food is arranged on a side table or in the kitchen, and guests help themselves.

- If your dining table is too small for the serving dishes and you don't want to do a buffet, you can plate-up individual servings in the kitchen and serve restaurant-style at the table. This tends to feel more formal and means a bit more work for you.

- Cocktails parties where the food and drinks are served standing up are great for a short period of time and a large number of people. They are especially good during busy times like the holidays or for pau hana (after-work) gatherings that are business related. These are perfect when you want to recognize a person or occasion, make contacts, and then move on. Remember that the drinks are the stars here, and the finger food should be able to be consumed in one or two bites.

# THE PARTIES

The parties in this book are meant to provide inspiration for you to do your own. Use them as a way to tickle your imagination and get you started. Holiday in Eden is an Epiphany party celebrated in January after the traditional Christmas season because the host and hostess are usually so busy in December to do it. The arrival of the wise men later on the epiphany seemed like a great solution.

Chinatown New Year was inspired by the desire to use a grandmother's canton dishes and shop the festival that is Chinatown during February. Two young women found a way to celebrate their Japanese heritage with a Girls' Day party that could just as easily be luncheon or tea.

Queen Emma Summer Palace raises funds to help maintain the property by renting out the adjacent hall and grounds for weddings and private parties. Their annual Pāpale Pāʻina held on the grounds was a natural trigger for a smaller private luncheon for friends.

The weather allows people throw parties in their backyards, or at the beach with regularity. One Oʻahu neighborhood's Easter brunch is becoming an annual event. Beach parties are wonderful almost anytime of the year. Add a weekend of camping and silly hats and it stands out. Just remember to bring mosquito spray and a jacket.

What all our partygivers have done here is take a typical island party and make it more special by giving it their own energy, details, and twist of style. These are not professional event planners. They are ordinary people who took the time.

# EASTER BRUNCH ON THE LAWN

# EASTER BRUNCH
## ON THE LAWN

Easter is about spring and renewal, decorating eggs and hunting them, bunnies and hats. Friends in one Nuʻuanu Valley neighborhood and their children opted for a mid-morning egg hunt and brunch followed by a rowdy game of croquet and a scavenger hunt up and down the street.

If Easter has a hue, it's pastel. It's also traditional foods, champagne, strawberries, asparagus, eggs, and all the bounty of the season. Even in Hawaiʻi, where those seasons are ever-so subtle, spring is in the air when Easter rolls around.

## Invitations

Because many of the neighbors have young children, making the invitations became an afternoon project. Seasonal cards were handmade with pastel construction paper and Easter bunny and egg stamps, then stuffed into pretty envelopes and placed in mailboxes.

If you don't have kids, the time, or the inclination, there are many store-bought invitations that work just fine. They can be handwritten or personalized on your home computer.

## Setting the Table

Pull tables outside on a lānai or backyard (remember to provide the shade of trees or umbrellas) where the adults can keep an eye on the children playing. Set a separate table for the children and give them their own indestructible decorations and tableware. Cover both tables with white linen tablecloths and layer with pastel tablecloths.

# What to Pour

## liliko'i spring sparkler
### SERVES 8

1 cup sugar
8 whole star anise
1 cup water
6 cups chilled liliko'i juice
1/3 cup Campari
2 cups chilled champagne

1. In a small saucepan, combine the sugar and star anise with 1 cup of water to make a simple syrup. Bring to a boil and stir until the sugar is dissolved.

2. Remove from the heat and cool. Discard the star anise, cover the syrup and store in the refrigerator. This can be made a day ahead.

3. In a large pitcher, combine the liliko'i juice, Campari and syrup. Chill.

4. Using champagne flutes or tall glasses, divide the juice mixture equally and top with champagne. If you prefer, you can add crushed ice to the glasses. Serve immediately.

At this party, the host and hostess pulled out their collection of highly collectible pastel Lu-Ray dishes from the 1940s, for a perfect Easter color scheme. Pink vintage glass vases filled with white roses, lemon leaves, and tiny pink blooms are placed down the center of the tables.

The children's table is decorated with less fragile objects such as wooden eggs, small tins of fresh daisies, and crêpe paper vegetables purchased at a party store.

Serve brunch family-style with dishes of food brought to the table. However, setting up a buffet table in the dining room or kitchen would work just as well. Set up the bar on a separate table or an island in the kitchen.

Set a separate table for the children and give them their own indestructible decorations and table-ware.

# ABOUT EASTER BASKETS

Before you run out to buy an Easter basket on sale, look around your house. It doesn't have to be the traditional pastel one you see everywhere. If it's a container, it can be an Easter basket. It can be an ethnic basket from an import store, a basket normally used as closet storage, one made of wire or sterling silver from Granny, or something that would look at home in a garden shop.

The traditional lau hala basket made from pandanus leaves would make a wonderful tropical statement, as would one crafted from coconut fronds.

One of the prettiest is a reproduction of an antique Japanese basket with a handle, filled with potted African violets from the garden shop and tied with a generous rose-colored grosgrain ribbon.

Think of the colors of spring when choosing ribbon and flowers—violet, rosy pink, baby blue, seafoam green, and soft yellow. Don't discount the use of polka dots and stripes either. Then stuff your basket with pretty moss, real grass, or interesting shredded excelsior. Skip the cellophane.

Top it off with pretty candy eggs, chocolate bunnies, and other seasonal candies. Treats and toys belong in your basket as well. If it's for an adult, consider tucking in a favorite CD, book, or movie tickets. Whatever you do, break open the treasure eggs of your imagination for fresh ideas.

## Attire

Ask everyone to wear croquet white, an Easter bonnet and come with a bottle of champagne. Have a stack of assorted hats available for guests to wear, collecting them early-on by borrowing from family and friends or scouring second-hand and discount stores.

## What to Do

On your lawn, set up a lively game or two of croquet (which gets much more spirited as the champagne flows). It's the ideal activity after brunch; or have chat time over cappuccinos. Ask the children to organize a neighborhood scavenger hunt and award prizes to the winners.

## Making It Easy

- Instead of the Liliko'i Spring Sparklers, serve popular Mimosas made with store-bought fresh orange juice topped with champagne and served in champagne flutes. Let your personal taste determine the proportions.

- Ready-to-go salads can be purchased and topped with your favorite bottled dressing. Fresh strawberries need only be washed and piled into bowls. Buy local ingredients from a Farmer's Market whenever possible.

- Croissants are readily-available in bakeries and most markets, and can be purchased frozen and simply baked just prior to serving.

- Cappuccino mixes are great if you don't have an espresso machine at home. The trick is beautiful presentation with whipped cream and nutmeg in generous mugs. Look for biscotti, the hard, twice-baked Italian cookie perfect for dipping, in any supermarket or specialty food store.

- A variety of ready-to-heat quiche can be found in the deli or frozen section of most markets. If you want to make them at home, pre-made crusts make it even simpler.

- If you don't want to be overwhelmed preparing food, assign dishes to guests and call it a potluck, or make one thing yourself and purchase the rest. There's a wide array of food available that makes entertaining easy. Besides being delicious, already-prepared food frees you to focus on other things. It's your choice.

# TIMELINE

**Three weeks:** If you are going to have neighborhood kids make invitations, gather them now for an arts and crafts afternoon. If not, look for invitations.

**Two weeks:** Mail the invitations. Look for a croquet set if you don't already own one.

**One week:** Hunt in your closets and on shelves for tablecloths, napkins and vases in a pastel, spring theme. If you don't have them, borrow from a friend, or shop inexpensive shops.

**Five days:** Check your closets for hats. Borrow them from friends if you have none.

**Three days:** Shop for groceries; purchase champagne.

**Two days:** Purchase the flowers. Set up or borrow folding tables and chairs if you are having a mob.

**One day:** Visit the local Farmer's market for fresh garden greens, fruit, baked goods and even locally grown coffee. Set the tables.

**When you wake:** Have a cup of coffee or tea and set to work making the quiches. Set up the bar and coffee station. Make the vinaigrette. Send someone out for ice.

**Two hours:** Set up the croquet game. Ice down the drinks and champagne.

**One hour:** Get dressed.

**During the party:** Warm the croissants, toss the salad and lay out a buffet table.

# menu

*liliko'i spring sparkler*

*salad of mānoa lettuce, goat
cheese, jicama, and pecans with
champagne vinaigrette*

*mushroom and swiss cheese
quiche*

*crabmeat quiche*

*fresh strawberries*

*warm croissants with pohā jam*

*cappuccino with nutmeg and
whipped cream*

*biscotti*

## crabmeat quiche

SERVES 6

3 tablespoons butter
3 tablespoons onion
6 ounces crabmeat, fresh or frozen
one 9-inch ready made pie crust
1 tablespoon grated Parmesan cheese
2 cups grated Swiss cheese
4 large eggs
1 cup heavy cream
1/4 teaspoon salt and dash of cayenne pepper

1. In a skillet, heat the butter and sauté the onion for a few minutes, until tender. Add the crabmeat and just heat through.

2. Place the pie crust into a pie dish, pressing it into the corners and crimping the edges.

3. Sprinkle the bottom of the pie shell with the Parmesan cheese. Layer with the crabmeat and onion mixture, and add the grated Swiss cheese on top.

4. In a bowl, mix the eggs, cream, salt, and cayenne pepper. Slowly pour over the pie ingredients.

5. Preheat the oven to 375°F degrees. Bake on the top rack of the oven until done, about 35 minutes. Check that the middle of the quiche has cooked. Do not overcook. Allow to cool a little before slicing.

*Cooked spinach, crumbled bacon, sautéed mushrooms, and cooked sausages can all be used instead of the crabmeat. Quiche is a very versatile dish.*

# salad of mānoa lettuce, goat cheese, jicama, and pecans with champagne vinaigrette

SERVES 6

1 head of Mānoa lettuce, washed and dried
2 ounces fresh goat cheese, cut into bite-sized pieces
1/2 cup jicama, peeled and cubed
1/2 cup whole pecans, toasted

CHAMPAGNE VINAIGRETTE:
3 tablespoons champagne vinegar
1/2 teaspoon Dijon mustard
1/2 teaspoon garlic, chopped
3/4 teaspoon salt
1/4 teaspoon pepper
1/2 cup olive oil

1. In a bowl, whisk together the vinegar, mustard, garlic, salt, and pepper. Slowly, while whisking, add the olive oil in a steady stream. Whisk until the dressing thickens and is emulsified.

2. Assemble the lettuce that has been torn into bite-sized pieces. Add the goat cheese, jicama, and pecans and toss right before serving. Adjust the ingredients to your preference.

# BOLLYWOOD BIRTHDAY

# BOLLYWOOD BIRTHDAY

What's a guy to do when his lovely, India-born wife's birthday is fast approaching and he has no ideas? He celebrates her heritage, of course. Larry and Amerjit Heim pulled out all the stops by inviting their friends to dress up and join the festivities by getting into the mood of the subcontinent.

In case you've never heard the term, Bollywood refers to the colorful, ebullient films starring gorgeous Indian actors who burst into song and dance at the most unexpected times.

The dinner was partially prepared by the couple and island chef Rohit Prasad who made the curry and other savory side dishes.

## Invitations

Make an invitation using an image from a Bollywood movie. You can download it online and set the party ambience well in advance. A good invitation will start the buzz about your party way before the day comes, so it's worth the effort.

"The contrived drama! The over-the-top acting! Wild dancing through every room!" this one read. Everyone was asked to come as a sexy Bollywood star complete with saris, turbans, and nose rings.

## Décor

Greet your guests as they did, with the candle glow of a walkway lined with gleaming white lanterns, which had been used previously at a charity event.

An intricately carved, wooden naga figure wearing tiny, sparkling votive candles on its back graced the home's entry table. A colorful ceramic bowl of voluptuous deep-pink peonies sat in front of it. Everywhere there were small glimmering votives in jewel-colored glass containers. Remember to make an impact when your guests first step in the door. If you cannot greet them yourself, delegate a friend to do it and introduce them to others.

In one corner of the living room set up a make-believe "hookah bar" by pulling together sofas and chairs filled with throw cushions that could have been purchased along the Silk Road. Even if your own furniture is hardly exotic, disguise it with dramatically patterned sheets or bedspreads. Section off the area with gossamer panels of multi-colored silk fabric suspended from the ceiling.

Project Bollywood movie classics on a blank wall and rotate them all evening long. The films can be rented from a video store or an online video rental service.

## Setting the Table

The table is set first with a blue linen tablecloth and then topped by a vivid garnet, embroidered Indian fabric. The same white lanterns that lined the walkway to the house sit on either end of the dining table lending a patterned magical glow during dinner.

The centerpiece of tropical Monsterra leaves and Birds-of-Paradise dominate the table. Fragrant fresh flowers and petals were scattered all over the table. Arrangements should be either very low or very high allowing guests to speak to those across the table.

Even if your own furniture
is hardly exotic, disguise it with dramatically
patterned sheets or bedspreads.

# What to Pour

*This is an unabashed tweak on the popular Cosmopolitan cocktail. Why not do the same and name a variation of a drink in honor of your occasion.*

### taj mahal

1 part Chambord
2 parts vodka
1 part pomegranate juice
a squirt of lime juice
honey
sugar
champagne to taste

1. In a tightly sealed cocktail shaker, combine the Chambord, vodka and juices with ice.

2. Shake until chilled and pour into prepared martini glasses.

3. Line the rims with honey and then dip into sugar before pouring. Top with champagne.

4. The Chambord, vodka, and juices can be made ahead and kept refrigerated in pitchers. You can skip the champagne altogether if you prefer.

## Favors

Pretty, shimmering silk gift bags from a local card shop hold small tins of saffron spice purchased in an Asian grocery. The bags were tied with a single fresh flower and placed at each guest's seat as a memento of the night. Be on the alert for inexpensive items to be used as favors. Often an entire event can be inspired by something this small.

## Making It Easy

- If you decide against serving cocktails, try a medium dry white wine or chilled beer with your samosas. Deep-frying samosas may be daunting to some, so substitute with ones ordered from an Indian restaurant or prepare wontons or lumpia(egg rolls) from the frozen food section of your local supermarket.

- Curry from scratch is best made a day ahead and refrigerated. You can make an even easier Japanese version with a curry mix found on supermarket shelves in the Asian food section. Just follow the directions and add meat or vegetables. While you are at the market, pick up a can of spicy chai tea mix and serve it warm after dinner.

- Forget the Bollywood movies. Instead visit your music store and check the international music section for CDs of Indian sitar music by someone like Ravi Shankar.

- Purchase a coconut cake from your favorite bakery, or substitute a combination of mango and coconut sorbet with good quality store-bought cookies.

- If you don't make chutney or know someone who does, pick up jars when you see them at church bazaars and school fairs.

# TIMELINE

**One month:** Order a sari and other pieces of Indian clothing such as jeweled slippers online.

**Three weeks:** Create your invitations and arrange to have them printed. Arrange to have help if necessary.

**Ten days:** Check your closets for colorful, exotic tableware and fabric to use in the décor. Shop for exotic Indian or Eastern music. Look for a projector for the films.

**One week:** Make sure you have lots of candles and votives. Prepare the samosas and freeze. Order the food from an Indian restaurant if you are not preparing it yourself.

**Three days:** Purchase the flowers and decorate the house. Set up the hookah bar area. Visit a video store if you are going to project Bollywood films on your walls.

**Two days:** Shop for groceries. Make the curry. Order the coconut cake.

**One day:** Set the table and check the flowers.

**Morning of:** Set up the bar. Purchase ice. Prepare the baked bananas and refrigerate for heating later. Prepare the chai and thaw the samosas.

**One hour:** Fry the samosas and keep warm in oven. Make the rice. Shower and dress.

**Just prior:** Light the candles. Turn on the music. Begin a movie on the wall (without sound). Have a Taj Mahal.

**During the party:** Bake the bananas, heat the curry, set out the condiments. Have fun.

**Arrange to sleep in late.**

# ABOUT HAWAIIAN CURRY

Curry has been a staple at Island tables for generations, albeit not the types commonly found in India. Instead, Island hostesses usually make a curry using chicken broth and coconut milk to which cooked chicken or shrimp is added.

Every year kama'āina families traditionally make chutney from the abundance of summer mangoes. Typically the meal also includes baked bananas, steamed rice, condiments, and coconut cake for dessert.

Curry does not refer to one dish, but rather to an entire genre of dishes that can be found throughout the Eastern hemisphere. It originated in India and, particularly during the nineteenth century, spread throughout the region. Never mistake the yellow powder purchased in supermarkets as "the real thing." It is used in this Hawaiian curry recipe because it is the one traditionally used in Hawai'i. However, the dish is improved if you add a tablespoon or so of the prepared curry pastes you find in Asian groceries.

You can find curries of all types in Thailand, Japan, Indonesia, Malaysia, and Sri Lanka. The English adopted curry through their colonization of this part of the world, and today practically think of it as a national dish. It usually contains meat, fish, or vegetables in a sauce and is served with rice, noodles, or the flat bread naan. In India there is also a "dry curry" made without sauce.

Curry mixes can be dry or moist. Most often the whole spices are warmed in a skillet to release their aroma, cooled, and then ground into a powder. A wet mixture may include ginger, chili, cilantro, and garlic ground together.

Common spice combinations are:

**Northern India and Pakistan**: Garam masala (masala means a spice blend), fresh cilantro, and ground or whole coriander seeds.

**Southern India**: fresh curry leaves, dried red chilies, split black lentils, mustard seeds.

**Thailand**: Thai basil, lemongrass, coconut milk, cilantro, Thai green chilies, palm sugar, kaffir lime leaves, Asian fish sauce.

**Singapore**: coconut milk, tamarind concentrate, cumin seeds, Thai basil, coriander seeds.

# menu

*taj mahal cocktails*

*samosas*

*hawaiian chicken
curry with chutney and
condiments*

*steamed jasmine rice*

*baked guava-
glazed bananas*

*coconut cake*

*masala chai tea*

# Recipes

## samosas

MAKES 20

one 14-ounce package large spring roll wrappers
2 large potatoes, cooked, peeled, and finely diced
1 tablespoon coriander seeds
1-1/2 teaspoons cumin seeds
1 teaspoon chili flakes

1/2 cup frozen peas, cooked
1 tablespoon fresh squeezed lemon juice
2 tablespoons chopped, fresh cilantro or mint
1/2 teaspoon salt
vegetable oil for frying

1. Set wrappers aside and cover with a cloth to keep moist.

2. Boil the potatoes until they can be pierced with a fork, about 10 minutes. Drain and cool until they can be peeled and diced.

3. In a dry skillet over medium heat, toast the coriander and cumin seeds until they are aromatic. Add the chili flakes and continue to toast.

4. Cool slightly and then grind the spices to a fine powder in a food grinder. A coffee grinder designated for spices works well. This can also be done with a simple mortar and pestle.

5. In a bowl, mix the potatoes, peas, spices, lemon juice, and chopped cilantro together. Salt to taste.

6. Carefully separate the wrappers and cut into 2- to 3-inch strips. Place a teaspoon of the filling mixture at one end of the strip.

7. Fold the wrapper over diagonally and continue to fold until the wrapper is used up and the shape is a stuffed triangle. Dampen the ends with water to seal the samosa. Continue until you have used up the wrappers and filling. You can freeze them between layers of waxed paper for later use.

8. Place the vegetable oil into a deep fryer or a heavy pan to a depth of 1- to 2-inches, or enough to comfortably fry the samosas. Heat the oil until very hot, but not boiling.

9. When you place the samosa in the oil, it should sizzle gently. Brown on both sizes and remove to a plate lined with paper towels.

10. Keep warm and serve with a sweet-chili sauce or mango chutney.

# hawaiian curry

SERVES 6

1/4 cup vegetable oil or butter (or a combination)
1 large onion, minced
1 red or green apple, peeled and diced
5 tablespoons flour
2 or more tablespoons of good curry powder
2 cups homemade or canned chicken stock
13.5 ounce can coconut milk (or a 12 ounce frozen bag)
2 cloves garlic
1/2 teaspoon salt
2 teaspoons fresh ginger, minced
2 cups cooked chicken or shrimp, cut into cubes

1. In a heavy saucepan, heat the oil and sauté the onions and apples. Cover and continue to cook until transparent, about 5 minutes.

2. Add the flour and curry powder to the mixture and continue to cook.

3. Slowly stir in the chicken stock and coconut milk.

4. Force the garlic through a garlic press and add it to the juice to the sauce.

5. Finally, add the salt and ginger. The sauce will thicken.

6. Taste for seasoning and add more curry powder if desired.

7. Cover and simmer over very low heat for 1 hour, stirring occasionally.

8. Add the cooked chicken or shrimp and continue cooking just long enough to heat it through.

9. Serve over rice with condiments such as mango chutney, chopped green onions, shredded coconut, chopped hard boiled eggs, chopped peanuts or macadamia nuts, raisins, or crisp, crumbled bacon.

# VERY PINK GIRLS' DAY

## VERY PINK GIRLS' DAY

Even big girls love tea parties, and Stacie Hurtado and Amy Lee of Mililani are no different. The two friends often give parties together saying that planning and shopping are more fun that way (and less exhausting). Both women have demanding jobs and find they have to plan their entertaining well in advance.

They begin with a theme or color scheme and build from there. Ideas come from everywhere: books, magazines, shopping sprees, and each other. Stacie says she likes to begin with what she already owns. They also borrow shamelessly from each other. She says that even though she has a color theme to work with, she doesn't think matching too much is a modern sensibility.

Their Very Pink party is ideal for a Japanese Girls' Day celebration, a baby shower, or birthday. It also moves nicely into the evening by adding cocktails, candles, and a few more dishes for the buffet.

The somen salad, sesame soy dressing, and namasu are homemade from family recipes. However, everything else, which is served cold, was purchased from a Japanese delicatessen and food shop. Assembling the food beautifully on pretty dishes makes it even more special.

## Invitations

With so many items already on the market, Stacie and Amy believe in purchasing items and personalizing them. For this event, blank cards were purchased at a stationery store, then the invitation written and customized by adding an outside cover of paper and a decorative flower stamp from a craft store. It was then placed in a colored envelope from a paper specialty shop.

## Favors

Waka-Cha tea soap by Eastern Accent fills the pretty-pink Asian take-out boxes on the hall console table and are ready to go when the party ends. Visit an Asian market or housewares store for paper and small gifts such as green tea candies or cookies to give as favors.

# What to Pour

## sakura punch

### SERVES 6

1 pint orange sherbet
3 cups pincapple juice
1 cup champagne or lemon-lime soda
orange slices for garnish

1. In a blender, put ice, sherbet, and pineapple juice.

2. Blend until smooth and pour into tall glasses.

3. Top with champagne to taste and mix gently to combine.

4. For a nonalcoholic drink, substitute with lemon-lime soda.

5. Garnish with a thin slice of fresh orange.

6. Serve immediately.

### ✦ ✦ ✦ NOTE ✦ ✦ ✦

*If you decide to serve punch in a punch bowl, combine the juices and chill them. Just before serving, add the champagne or soda. Float scoops of the sherbert on top of the punch.*

## Setting the Table

Stacie and Amy agree that layering and texture give a table more interest. Here they begin with a hot pink tablecloth and top it with felt fiber wrapping paper purchased from an online site. The top layer is a silk obi borrowed from one of Stacie's friends.

The clear glass vases were purchased inexpensively at Wal-Mart and filled with paper flowers and branches found in the accessories department of a local furniture store. The placemats are from Pier 1 Imports. The glasses (etched with a cherry blossom motif) are filled with a refreshing lemon-lime soda and topped with grenadine.

Pretty rice cakes—layered in white for purity, pink for the flowers of spring, and green for summer—are served at this time.

# DOS & DON'TS OF SUSHI

- It is okay to pick up sushi with either hashi (chopsticks) or your fingers.

- If soy sauce is offered, dip the sushi on the fish side into a small amount of sauce. Don't double dip.

- Sushi should be eaten in one or two bites depending on the size.

- When eating sushi from a shared platter, use the blunt end of the chopsticks to pick it up and place it on your own plate. Eat with the pointed ends.

- When you are not using your chopsticks, place them on the small ceramic holder provided. When you are finished eating, place the chopsticks across the soy sauce dish.

- Don't rub your chopsticks together to get rid of splinters. This is an insult in a good sushi bar.

- Eat the ginger provided as a palate cleanser. Do not plop it on top of the sushi.

- This may be a big surprise, but you shouldn't mix wasabi with the soy sauce. Wasabi should be placed inside the sushi when being prepared. If wasabi is not to your taste, let the sushi chef know.

- Do not hand money directly to the sushi chef. He should not touch money while he is preparing sushi.

# HINA MATSURI (GIRLS' DAY)

March third is a special day set aside for Japanese and Okinawan girls each year. Traditionally, girls unpack their collection of dolls that was begun at birth and place them for display in their home. The dolls, including likenesses of the emperor and empress, wear costumes from the Heian period (794-1185 A.D.), which was considered a high point in Japanese culture.

Pretty rice cakes called hishi mochi—layered in white for purity, pink for the flowers of spring, and green for summer—are served at this time. Other traditional dishes include sekihan (red beans with rice), ochagash (tea cakes), and umani (meat and vegetables). Girls also receive paper peach blossoms symbolizing the hope that there will be calm and tranquility in their lives.

## menu

*assorted sushi*

*fresh 'ahi sashimi*

*edamame*

*cold grilled salmon*

*nishime*

*tofu with bonito flakes and
ponzu sauce*

*somen salad with sesame soy
dressing*

*namasu and assorted tsukemono*

*mochi and manju*

# Recipes

## cold somen salad
### SERVES 8

one 9-ounce package somen noodles

SAUCE:
1/4 cup sugar
1 cup chicken broth or dashi *
1/4 cup soy sauce
1/4 cup rice vinegar
2 tablespoons sesame oil

GARNISH:
1 small cucumber, peeled, seeded, julienned
2 cups shredded iceberg lettuce
7 ounces (half block) kamaboko,* julienned
1/4 pound of ham, julienned
2 eggs, beaten, cooked, cooled and julienned
1/4 pound char siu, cut into small pieces
1/4 cup minced green onions

1. Cook the somen noodles according to the package directions. Drain and rinse, then set aside to cool in the refrigerator.

2. In a saucepan over medium-high heat, combine the ingredients for the sauce. Bring to a boil, then reduce to simmer and continue to cook for another 5 minutes. Set aside and chill.

3. Prepare the garnishes.

4. Place the eggs into a bowl and scramble with a fork. Pour into a greased sauté pan and cook like a pancake, turning once. Cool the egg "omelet" on a plate, then cut into julienne strips.

5. To assemble the platter, place the chilled noodles on the bottom. Place the garnishes in groupings on top and cover the noodles. Serve the sauce on the side, or pour over just prior to serving.

*Dashi is a Japanese soup broth that can be purchased ready made in the Asian section of a market.
*Kamaboko is fishcake. Several different kinds are also available in Asian markets.

# simple cucumber namasu

### SERVES 6

2 large cucumbers, peeled, seeded, and sliced thin
1/2 onion, sliced thin
1 small can smoked baby oysters, optional

SAUCE:
1 cup rice vinegar
1/4 cup sugar
Salt and pepper to taste
1 tablespoon soy sauce

1. Prepare the vegetables by slicing them very thin and placing them in a bowl.

2. In another bowl, combine the sauce ingredients and stir until the sugar is dissolved.

3. Pour the mixture over the vegetables and refrigerate to combine flavors for 1 to 2 hours.

4. Prior to serving, drain and add the smoked baby oysters. Serve as an edible garnish.

Nishime, pictured, can be purchased ready made.

# TIMELINE

**Three weeks:** Create invitations. Put them in the mail.

**Two weeks:** Order favors online, or look for them in import and candy shops.

**One week:** Check your closets for all things pink and Asian. Borrow from family and friends.

**Three days:** Pick up fresh flowers and paper goods.

**Two days:** Shop for groceries for the tofu dish and somen salad. Order special mochi and sushi.

**One day:** Set the table. Purchase the nishime, salmon, edamame, sashimi. Make the somen salad and tofu. Set up the bar, if you are having one.

**Morning of:** Pick up mochi and sushi.

**15 minutes:** Make the punch.

**During the party:** Heat the food and set up the buffet.

# BEACH PARTY GOES TEX MEX

# BEACH PARTY GOES TEX MEX

What better way to enjoy summer in Hawai'i than at the beach. Interior designer Jonathan Staub and writer Jeff Finney decided against the expected Hawaiian lū'au and instead chose to serve up tacos, rice, and beans from a Wai'anae restaurant along with Mexican beers and margaritas. The private beachfront property was once the home of Staub's great-grandmother and a place filled with happy childhood memories. Friends were invited to bring their children, wear festive headgear, and camp overnight at the site. Did I mention that the invitations were written in Spanish? So it was every man for himself.

## Setting the Table

Set up a long dining table with white folding chairs placed on both sides. This creates a lively, friendly feeling. Cover the table with a hot pink tablecloth and top it with a stripped Mexican runner down the center of the table. Place tall metal containers filled with brightly colored Mexican paper flowers purchased from a local Mexican grocery and tropical green leaves on the runner.

Rustic bottle-shaped hurricanes (lamps) hold votive candles and are placed at close intervals down the table. Scattered among the hurricanes are individually wrapped Mexican candies, an after-dinner treat. Lighting is critical when having an outdoor party; have someone string lines in trees to illuminate your site.

The bar and buffet tables are decorated with Mexican paper flowers, papier mâché fruit, napkins, and plastic cups and plates in hot Latin colors. (This is one of those times to use paper and plastic.) Strung everywhere are Mexican paper cutout banners and national flags, which can be ordered online. Nature's awesome sunset and good friends take care of the rest.

## Making It Easy

+ If you don't have access to a private beach, why not throw a fiesta in your backyard complete with piñatas for the kids? It takes care of the issue of electricity for blending margaritas and chafing dishes for the warm picadillo and tortillas.

*...throw a fiesta in your backyard complete with piñatas for the kids...*

# What to Pour

## mango margarita

### MAKES 2 DRINKS

*This is a wonderful, refreshing twist on the classic margarita.*
*Summer is mango season, and what better way to celebrate it.*

1-1/2 ounces white tequila
1/2 ounce triple sec
1/2 fresh mango, peeled and diced, or 2 ounces frozen mango
3-1/2 ounces sweet & sour mix
margarita salt
lime juice

1.  If you have access to electricity at the beach, you can place all the ingredients, including fresh mango, into a blender filled with ice and pour into a margarita glass with a salted rim. Use the mango purée if you do not have a blender on hand. Shake all ingredients over ice and pour into iced tumblers.

2.  To make the salt rim, put coarse or margarita salt in a flat dish. Rub fresh lime juice around the rim of the glass and invert into the salt. Pour and serve immediately.

# ono tequila sparkler
### MAKES 1 DRINK

*This simple mixed cocktail is great for a
hot day—and a snap to make.*

1 ounce white tequila
1 ounce fresh squeezed lime juice
4 ounces lemon-lime soda
sprig of coriander

1. Fill a tumbler with ice, tequila, lime juice, and soda and stir.

2. Garnish with a sprig of coriander.

# mexican beer

1. Fill a cooler with ice and assorted Mexican beers available in most supermarkets.

2. If you have a Mexican grocery in your neighborhood, add the fruit-flavored sodas so popular south of the border.

# OUTDOOR DINING

## Here are some tips for entertaining outdoors.

- If you are at the beach, remember to have sunscreen on hand for anyone who has forgotten to bring it—especially for the children. Mosquito repellent is also a good idea.

- Entertaining at night means you need to consider outdoor lighting. If there is no access to electrical outlets, make sure you have enough hurricanes. Place them everywhere, including hanging them from the trees.

- Expect mosquitoes. Citronella candles or mosquito punks are a must.

- Even in Hawai'i, evenings at the beach can get cool. Make sure you ask guests to bring sweatshirts, sweaters, or shawls. Plan to have extras for those who have forgotten them.

- Folding lawn chairs and hammocks are great to have scattered around for people to collapse on and visit with each other. Have them face the water and the sunset.

- Keep outdoor food simple, and make sure there is plenty of ice in the coolers. Planning is everything when you take a party outside. Serve food you can eat at room temperature and without knives.

- Beaches are often windy. Anchor the tablecloth by tying beach rocks or coral to the ends. Have a Plan B in case the weather turns bad quickly. Also, eating in the hot sun can be unbearable. Provide the shade of a tree, tent, tarp, or umbrellas.

- In the backyard, galvanized tubs from the hardware store make great containers to chill beer, wine, and soft drinks. Just fill with ice and a little water. Wheelbarrows and tote bags are great for holding anything from disposable cameras to party favors and chips.

- Place the buffet table near the kitchen, if you have one, and the dining tables away from the buffet to avoid a logjam.

## menu

*mango margaritas*

*mexican seviche*

*guacamole and tortilla chips*

*build-a-taco bar*

*pico de gallo salad*

*cornbread*

*tropical fruit sorbets*

*caramel flan*

# Recipes

## mexican seviche

SERVES 6

*Any very fresh fish works for seviche. Select from the freshest available.*

2 pounds fresh fish fillets,
cut into 1-inch cubes
3/4 cup freshly squeezed lemon juice
1 medium sweet onion, chopped
4 large tomatoes, seeded and chopped
1/2 cup fresh cilantro, chopped
1/2 cup vegetable oil
1/2 fresh Jalapeno pepper, seeded and chopped, or to taste
1/2 teaspoon dried oregano, or 1 tablespoon fresh chopped
Salt and pepper to taste

4 Haas avocados, coarsely chopped

1. Place the fish in a non-reactive bowl and pour enough lemon juice over it to cover.

2. Refrigerate an hour or so, or long enough to have the fish begin to turn partially white.

3. Drain off the juice and add the onion, tomatoes, cilantro, oil, pepper, and oregano.

4. Salt and pepper to taste.

5. When you are ready to eat, add the avocados. Mix and serve immediately.

# build-a-taco bar
*This is a matter of assemblage.*

1. Buy the best quality soft, corn tortillas you can. They are available fresh or frozen in most Mexican markets.

2. Make a picadillo (recipe on page 93), or meat sauce.

3. Chop lettuce and tomatoes.

4. Grate the cheese.

5. Other condiments you can add are fresh salsa, refried beans, sour cream, chopped olives, chilies ,and hot sauce. Keep the picadillo warm, if possible. Assemble all the ingredients in separate dishes and let your guests build their own tacos.

# pico de gallo salad
### SERVES 6

2 cups jicama, peeled and cut into cubes
4 oranges, peeled and cut into cubes
1/4 cup fresh lime juice
1/4 teaspoon sea salt
powdered paprika or Mexican chili powder, to taste

1. In a bowl, mix the jicama, oranges, lime juice, and sea salt.

2. Refrigerate for 3 hours.

3. Before serving, sprinkle with the paprika or chili powder.

# TIMELINE

**Four to six weeks:** Secure the venue. Check if there are any necessary permits for a public facility such as a beach or park. Rent a beach house.

**One month:** Create the invitations and have them printed, if necessary. Secure a caterer if you do not plan a potluck or to make the food yourself.

**Two to three weeks:** Mail invitations with parking instructions and map if necessary. Check out stores for bright plastic plates, paper napkins, and glasses. Look online for piñatas and banners.

**Ten days:** Rent or borrow portable tables and chairs, if necessary. Arrange to have them taken to the site, if not your own backyard.

**One week:** Order a cake if this is a special occasion.

**Three days:** Visit a Hispanic market for candies and food specialties. Purchase mangoes and avocados if they need to ripen.

**Two days:** Shop for groceries if you have not hired a caterer. Buy the tequila and beer.

**One day:** Purchase the fish for the seviche. Prepare the food.

**Morning of the party:** Make the cornbread. Purchase ice.

**One to three hours:** Pack the food in coolers if you are going to a public site. Arrive early and set up decorations. Set up tables for the food and bar. Ice the beer.

**One hour:** Hang the piñatas. Mix the margaritas. Start the charcoal if you are grilling anything.

# picadillo

*This recipe was adapted from the book* Frida's Fiestas,
*a collection of recipes from famed Mexican artist Frida Kahlo. She used pork and lard in the original recipe which have been substituted here. Kahlo stuffed the mixture into poblano chilies. I have also added spices and sugar used by Mexican culinary expert Diana Kennedy in her version of the dish.*

3 pounds ground beef or pork
1 large onion, cut in half
3 cloves garlic, chopped
2 whole cloves
1 cinnamon stick
salt and pepper to taste
6 tablespoons olive oil
1 small onion, finely chopped
3 carrots, peeled and finely chopped
2 zucchini, finely chopped
1/3 cup flat leaf parsley, chopped
1 pound chopped tomatoes
1 teaspoon sugar
3/4 cup almonds, chopped
1/2 cup golden raisins

1. In a skillet, sauté the meat and onion halves, garlic, cloves, cinnamon, and salt and pepper until cooked, about 20 minutes. Drain the fat and discard the onion.

2. In another pan, heat the olive oil and sauté the chopped onion, carrots and zucchini until the onion is translucent. Add the parsley, tomato, sugar, almonds, raisins and meat.

3. Correct seasoning, lower the heat to simmer and continue to cook until the mixture thickens and the tomato is cooked through, about 20 minutes. Use to fill the soft, warmed tacos.

# TAKE IT TO A TEAHOUSE

# TAKE IT TO A TEAHOUSE

When you want to throw a party but don't have the room, time, or inclination to clean up afterward, then take it to a restaurant or, in this case, an 85-year-old teahouse high above Honolulu. That's what interior designer Marion Philpotts Miller and her husband, attorney Jeff Miller, did with fantastic results. Check your own neighborhood for a classic old establishment that allows you lots of flexibility and serves good food.

Natsunoya Teahouse is one of the last of its kind in Hawai'i. Once a vital social element in the local Japanese community, it allows you to bring your own bartender and liquor which can be a substantial savings. You also have the freedom to decorate as you please which, of course, pleased the Millers. Don't expect the same flexibility with most other restaurants. However, you will be surprised how many places are willing to work with you, especially if they have a private dining room.

This Tatami Room is classically and sparely furnished with three tokunomas (niches) on one side. The Millers supplemented with their own artwork and flowers from home.

## Invitations

Because this party was hastily put together to celebrate Marion's birthday, the invitations, complete with the teahouse logo and map, went out as e-mails. If you'd rather send a written one, choose from the multitude of Asian-inspired, ready-made cards at specialty card shops, then personalize the invitation. Send them out two to three weeks ahead of your event.

## Setting the Table and Favors

Blue and white, a favorite color combination in Japanese country interiors, is accented with yellow. The teahouse set up a long, low table flanked on both sides with bentwood seats with cushions. Napkins are folded and placed into wine glasses and match the restaurant's standard white tablecloths. Many places offer a choice of colored napkins, or you can throw on colorful pieces of fabric or runners to create a color theme.

Marion Philpotts Miller scoured an inexpensive import store and found miniature rustic containers with the right aesthetic. Small yellow chrysanthemums purchased at a local wholesaler were cut short and placed in the containers. Marion then ran them down the length of the table.

Small Japanese ceramic tea cups which could be used as flower containers, were also found and presented as favors in bags made of woven straw and fabric and placed at each seat.

Inspired by the décor, the owner of the teahouse and her friend provided the party with small, handmade origami birds for good luck. The wooden chopsticks were removed from their wrappings and placed at each setting. Teahouse staff then set the table with blue and white Japanese plates and sake cups from their own stock to further the color scheme.

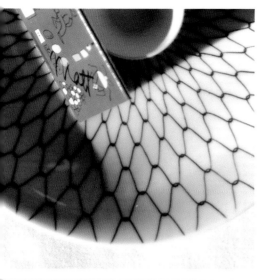

## Music to Play

Because a sound system is non-existent in the old teahouse, Japanese pop and jazz tunes were downloaded to an ipod and played through the ipod's portable speakers.

Rent or borrow a karaoke machine so everyone can sing the rest of the night away after dinner. It's a great way to end an evening of food and drink "on the floor."

## Making It Easy

- It can't get much easier than holding your event at a restaurant. The setting, food, and clean up are part of the package. If you decide to have a party in a home setting and want to keep it simple, consider ordering take-out from a favorite restaurant. If you prefer making some dishes yourself, recipes are provided at the end of the chapter.

- To top off the meal, order dessert such as a chocolate green tea torte from among several excellent Japanese-style Island bakeries, or serve mochi ice cream, which is available in most markets in Hawai'i.

*Send invitations out two to three weeks ahead of your event.*

# What to Pour

*These two festive recipes were provided by Randy Kubo,*
*the importer of an Okinawan liquor called awamori, which is distilled from rice.*
*Vodka is a good substitute for awamori.*

## enlightment

### MAKES 1 DRINK

1 ounce awamori or vodka
1 ounce Midori melon liqueur
2 to 3 lime wedges, squeezed

1. Place all ingredients into a cocktail shaker filled with ice.

2. Shake three or four times.

3. Strain into a chilled martini glass.

## karma

### MAKES 1 DRINK

1 ounce awamori or vodka
1/3 ounce triple sec
1 ounce cranberry juice
2 to 3 lime wedges, squeezed

1. Place all ingredients into a cocktail shaker filled with ice; shake three or four times.

2. Strain into a chilled martini glass.

# TIMELINE

**Four to six weeks:** Select a place to hold your party. Secure the date. Talk to the manager to find out what is expected and what they will provide. Arrange any special floral arrangements, the menu, music, bar set up, and special drinks.

**Three weeks:** Mail the invitations.

**One week:** Confirm arrangements with the restaurant.

**Day of:** Arrive an hour early to check the table, music, flowers, and menu selections. If it's a party with gifts, make sure there is a table set up for them. Confirm arrangements for payment.

**15 minutes:** Relax and order a drink.

**Party begins:** Greet your guests and enjoy.

# HOW-TOS OF A RESTAURANT PARTY

There are lots of reasons for having your party in a restaurant: little or no clean-up, great food, enough space to accommodate guests. It doesn't have to cost a lot either. Choose an upscale establishment with a private dining room if you can afford it. You can have equally as much fun in an inexpensive restaurant if you look around. Here are some tips when entertaining outside the home.

- Decide if you're paying for it yourself, or if the cost will be shared by others. If costs are shared, assign one person to be in charge of working with the restaurant and assigning tasks such as flowers or place cards. Make sure everyone can afford the restaurant that's been chosen.

- The person paying the bill should send the invitations. If it's a group, decide whether the group wants them mailed, or sent via emails with follow-up phone calls. Try to get them out at least three weeks prior to the event.

- About the same time, visit the restaurant to select the room or table you want to use. Determine what they can provide, such as tablecloths, napkins and wine glasses. Are you bringing your own tablecloth toppers, votives, or flowers? Let the restaurant know how you want to embellish their setting.

- Keep in mind that the establishment will need a head count by a cut-off date. If there are more than eight people, consider having a pre-set menu. Offer a choice of meat or fish, and make sure you provide for vegetarians.

- Most bakeries do a better job at birthday cakes (if that's what you're celebrating) than restaurants. Order ahead and make sure the restaurant allows them to be brought in.

- Consider where guests will gather for pre-dinner drinks. Is there room in the private room, or will you meet in a part of the bar? Let both the restaurant and guests know if it's a host or no-host bar. If you bring your own wine, expect to be charged a corkage fee.

- Show up an hour prior to the party to check table settings, make sure candles are lit, and have the bar ready for the first arrivals. If the private room does not have music, ask if you can bring in an ipod and speakers, or hire a guitarist or pianist.

- One more thing: make arrangements to settle the bill discreetly. Avoid collecting money or discussing the bill in front of guests. If you are paying, it's best to quietly slip away.

# menu

*appetizers served at the bar*
*assorted sushi and 'ahi sashimi*

*wasabi macadamia nuts and japanese crackers*

*small platters served at the table*
*nalo greens with soy sesame dressing*

*miso ahi steaks*

*minced chicken with lettuce cups*

*namasu*

*miso soup*

*rice*

*individual mochi ice cream balls*

# Recipes

*These Asian-inspired dishes are simple to make at home. Serve with hot rice.*

## miso ʻahi steaks

### SERVES 6

1/3 cup water
2/3 cup white miso paste
1 teaspoon soy sauce
2 tablespoons or less brown sugar
3 pieces fresh ginger (the size of a quarter), peeled and minced, about 2 teaspoons
6 fresh ʻahi steaks
3 tablespoons oil for cooking
2 tablespoons minced chives, green onions, or cilantro
salt and pepper to taste

1. In a small saucepan, combine the water, miso paste, soy sauce, brown sugar, and ginger.

2. Cook over medium heat, stirring until the sugar has dissolved.

3. In a skillet, heat the cooking oil and sauté the ʻahi steaks for 2 or 3 minutes on each side, until lightly browned.

4. Pour the miso mixture over the ʻahi steaks and simmer over medium heat for another 2 to 3 minutes. Do not overcook.

5. Remove ʻahi to a serving dish and sprinkle with the chives, green onions, or cilantro.

# minced chicken with lettuce cups

## SERVES 6

*This has been adapted from one of James McNair's recipes.*
*Similar dishes are served in many Southeast Asian restaurants.*

1 head iceberg lettuce
6 dried Chinese black mushrooms
3 tablespoons toasted sesame seeds
5 chicken thighs, boneless and skinless
2 tablespoons oyster sauce
1 tablespoon soy sauce
1 tablespoon dry sherry or bourbon
1 tablespoon sugar
1/4 cup peanut oil
2 chopped green onions
1-1/2 inch piece fresh ginger, peeled and minced
3/4 cup canned water chestnuts, minced
1 teaspoon sesame oil
1 teaspoon cornstarch, mixed with 2 tablespoons water
salt and pepper to taste
plum sauce, optional

1. Wash, separate, rinse, and dry the lettuce leaves. Set aside in the refrigerator until ready to serve.

2. Place the dried mushrooms in a bowl with warm water and allow to hydrate for about 2 hours.

3. Drain and squeeze out the water.

4. Cut off the stems and chop finely. Set aside.

5. Toast the sesame seeds in a dry skillet for about 5 minutes, or until lightly browned. Do not burn. Set aside.

6. Mince the chicken thighs into small pieces and set aside.

7. In a small bowl, combine the oyster sauce, soy sauce, sherry, or bourbon and sugar. Stir to dissolve the sugar and set aside.

8. Heat a wok or skillet with 1/4 cup peanut oil and coat the bottom of the pan. When the skillet is quite hot, sauté the minced chicken, green onions, and ginger for about 2 minutes.

9. Add the water chestnuts and mushrooms and quickly sauté another 2 minutes.

10. Add the sesame oil, sesame seeds, oyster sauce mixture, and cornstarch mixed with water. The sauce will thicken quickly, about another 1 or 2 minutes.

11. Season with salt and pepper and transfer to a serving dish.

12. To eat, fill the lettuce "cups" with the mixture and wrap to eat. You may want to first spread a little plum sauce on the lettuce leaf for a sweeter taste.

# PALACE PĀPALE PĀʻINA

# PALACE PĀPALE PĀʻINA

Pāpale is the Hawaiian word for hat. Pāʻina is a luncheon. Each year the Daughters of Hawaiʻi throw a Pāpale Pāʻina for their membership and ask them to wear hats, most of them traditional lau hala, and join each other for lunch at Queen Emma Summer Palace on the Pali Highway. The Daughters, busy young attorneys and mothers, spend a couple of hours filled with laughter and good food under the trees on the palace grounds.

While often thought of as remnants of another era, ladies' luncheons can still be a fun way to reconnect with the girls and spend time away from the pressures of modern life.

## Invitations and Favors

Search specialty stationery shops for cards or note paper with hats printed on them. They are more available than you think. You can also find small straw hats in craft shops or some department stores. Hot glue them onto blank cards and write in the party information. If you hold your luncheon at a place that has a gift shop, look for logo items that you can use as invitations and favors.

## Setting the Table

Because this is a ladies' luncheon and not a lūʻau, the table is set with a bisque-colored tablecloth and white napkins with a coral design embroidered on them. Find cloth napkins that are reminiscent of your setting or complement your color scheme. We used bamboo-handled flatware and lau hala napkin rings. Blue and rust hydrangea were purchased from a local floral wholesaler and the stems cut short. Inexpensive, white ceramic flower pots fitted inside with a plastic cup to hold water serve as vases.

# What to Pour

### emalani cocktail
#### SERVES 6

1 cup white rum
1/2 cup triple sec
1/2 cup fresh orange juice
1/2 cup fresh lime juice
1/2 cup simple syrup
lemon-lime soda to taste
pineapple spear and mint for garnish

1. In a pitcher, combine the rum, triple sec, juices, and simple syrup.

2. Fill tall glasses with ice cubes and pour in the juice mixture leaving room for the soda.

3. Top with the soda and stir.

4. Garnish the drinks with a spear of pineapple and sprig of mint. (Vodka can be substituted for the rum).

### ◆ ◆ ◆ N O T E ◆ ◆ ◆

*Make simple syrup by placing 1 cup of sugar and 1/2 cup of water into a saucepan. Simmer until all the sugar is dissolved and the mixture is clear. Cool and refrigerate until ready to use.*

## Making It Easy

+ Serve fresh fruit cocktails with mint as a first course. It's downright retro and refreshing.

+ Instead of the roast duck and portobello mushroom salad, assemble a classic Chinese chicken salad with packaged greens, wonton chips, mandarin oranges, slivered almonds, and roasted chicken from the store, topped off with bottled Asian-style dressing.

+ Purchase a coconut cake from your favorite bakery for dessert, or serve fruit sorbet and your favorite store-bought shortbread cookies.

## Music to Play

Anything by Na Leo Pilimehana, Israel Kamakawiwoʻole's "Facing Future," or Hoʻokena's "Thirst Quencher."

# TIMELINE

**Three weeks:** Create invitations and mail.

**One week:** Rent tables and chairs if necessary. Order the duck.

**Three days:** Check table linens and dishes. Wash or purchase extras if necessary.

**Two days:** Buy everything for drinks and groceries, except the roast duck.

**One day:** Make carrot ginger soup and haupia squares. Pick up fresh flowers.

**Morning of:** Pick up duck and make salad and iced tea. Make table arrangements.

**Two hours:** Transport tables, chairs, cooler, and food to the site. Arrange to have the tables and chairs delivered if you have rented them. Set the table.

**One hour:** Set up the tableware. Set up the music.

**When guests arrive:** Pour the drinks, start the music.

# THE QUEEN'S RETREAT

Queen Emma Summer Palace sits tucked up on a hill behind tropical foliage barely visable to cars flying past on the Pali Highway below. All a person has to do is head up the driveway and park beneath the mango and kukui trees to feel they've entered a quiet, much gentler world. The traffic sounds fall by the wayside as cool breezes rustle the tall, old trees. The stately house sits proudly and serenely with its forest green trimmed shutters and graceful white columns.

The original palace was a prefab, Regency-style kit home sent around the Horn from Boston in 1848 and was erected a few miles from downtown Honolulu. The original owner was in the home a matter of months before he sold it to John Young II, also known as Keoni Ana, the part-Hawaiian son of one of King Kamehameha's most trusted friends. The home eventually came to Young's niece, Queen Emma, who used it as a retreat from the dust and heat of the town.

It was a place for the king, queen, and their small son to be a regular family. When both the king and young prince died within a year of each other, the queen spent many days in mourning at the palace. In later years she used the home for elegant parties and entertaining, even adding on an entire room to entertain the visiting Duke of Edinburgh.

In 1890, the Hawaiian government purchased the property from the Queen's estate. It was destined to be demolished to make way for a baseball field when it was rescued by the Daughters of Hawai'i, a group of strong-willed ladies who also happened to be married to some of the town's most influential men.

The Daughters continue to operate the palace today as a museum and popular place to hold events and weddings. Proceeds from the rentals help maintain the palace and grounds.

# menu

*emalani cocktail*

*ginger carrot soup*
*with taro rolls*

*chinese roast duck and grilled*
*portobello mushroom salad with*
*balsamic vinaigrette*

*hilo haupia squares*

*fresh kona coffee*

*spicy hawaiian*
*iced tea*

# Recipes

## ginger carrot soup

### SERVES 8

*There are many versions of this soup. This one is a variation of a recipe from chef Sam Choy and can be served hot or cold. He suggests strips of carrot and ginger as a garnish, but I prefer chopped fresh cilantro.*

1/2 cup chopped onion
1/4 cup peeled, minced fresh ginger
1/4 teaspoon cinnamon
1/8 teaspoon nutmeg
2 tablespoons good oil
1 quart chicken stock
1-1/2 pounds carrots, peeled and chopped

1 cup half-and-half
1 cup fresh orange juice
1 tablespoon dry sherry
3 tablespoons butter
3 tablespoons flour
salt and pepper to taste
1/4 cup chopped cilantro for garnish

1. In a large saucepan, sauté the onion, ginger, cinnamon, and nutmet in oil until the onions are transparent, about 5 minutes.

2. Add the chicken stock and carrots and bring to a boil then reduce and simmer for about 25 or 30 minutes, until the carrots are done.

3. Remove from the stove and cool slightly.

4. Working in batches, purée the carrot mixture in a blender until smooth.

5. Return the purée to the saucepan and add the half-and-half, orange juice, and sherry.

6. Continue to cook over medium-low heat for 5 minutes.

7. In another saucepan, melt the butter and add the flour, stir and cook for about 3 or 4 minutes to make a roux.

8. Add the carrot mixture slowly to the butter and flour and stir until smooth and thickened. Season with salt and pepper. This can be made a day ahead and kept in the refrigerator to deepen the flavors.

9. Serve hot or cold with cilantro as a garnish.

# chinese roast duck and grilled portobello mushroom salad with balsamic vinaigrette

## SERVES 8

*If you live near a Chinatown, buy an already-prepared duck and bring it home to debone. You can also use two boneless duck breasts roasted with salt and pepper for about 20 minutes in a 400-degree oven. Chicken is a good substitute for the duck if you can't get it.*

### MARINADE AND DRESSING:
1/3 cup light brown sugar
1/2 cup balsamic vinegar
2 cups extra virgin olive oil
Salt and pepper to taste
2 portabello mushrooms

1. Mix the sugar, balsamic vinegar, olive oil, and seasonings together.

2. Use 1/3 cup for the marinade and save the rest for the salad dressing.

3. Place the mushrooms in a plastic bag or nonreactive bowl and marinate with the dressing at least two hours, or overnight in the refrigerator.

4. Before preparing the salad, grill the mushrooms for about 5 to 10 minutes on each side, or until they are cooked through and have grill marks.

### SALAD:
1 Chinese roast duck, cooked and deboned, cut into slices
2 stalks scallions or green onions, sliced on the diagonal
1 red or yellow bell pepper, sliced into strips
1 Japanese cucumber, peeled, seeded, and cut into diagonal slices
2 cups mesclun salad greens
1 cup toasted almonds, slivered
2 oranges, peeled, sliced in half
1/2 pint fresh blueberries or raspberries

1. In a salad bowl, assemble the roast duck, green onions, peppers, cucumber, greens, almonds, oranges, and berries.

2. Toss lightly with some of the reserved dressing. You will have leftover dressing for another day.

3. Slice the grilled mushrooms and place the strips on top of the salad then serve immediately.

# hilo haupia squares

## SERVES 12

*This is also an adaptation of a chef Sam Choy dessert. You will have leftovers and be delighted the next day when you discover them in the refrigerator. I prefer making it with Hawaiian coconut milk that has been frozen fresh than the heavier and sweeter Asian variety in cans. If you can only get the canned variety, use less sugar. If you don't want to make the haupia from scratch, use one of the quick mixes on the market.*

CRUST:
1 cup butter, softened
2 cups flour
1/3 cup light brown sugar
1/2 cup finely chopped macadamia nuts

FILLING:
two 12-ounce cans coconut milk, frozen and thawed
1-1/2 cups whole milk
3/4 cup water
1 cup or less sugar
1/2 cup cornstarch

TOPPING:
1 cup toasted coconut flakes
one 8-ounce can crushed pineapple

1. Preheat the oven to 350°F.

2. In a mixing bowl, use a pastry blender to cut the butter and flour.

3. Stir in the brown sugar and nuts.

4. Press the mixture into a 9x13-inch baking pan.

5. Bake for 15 to 20 minutes, or until light brown. Remove and cool on a rack.

6. In a saucepan over medium heat, combine the coconut milk, whole milk, and water.

7. Mix together the sugar and cornstarch and add to the mixture.

8. Bring to a boil, reduce the heat to simmer and continue to cook, stirring regularly to avoid lumps until the haupia thickens, about 5 minutes.

9. Pour the warm mixture over the cooled crust. Cool and then refrigerate to set.

10. Before serving, cut into squares and sprinkle each piece with toasted coconut and a dollop of crushed pineapple.

*You will have leftovers and be delighted the next day when you discover them in the refrigerator.*

# SURPRISE BABY SHOWER AT THE OFFICE

# SURPRISE BABY SHOWER AT THE OFFICE

The pau hana office party is an established institution in the Islands, as are potlucks. So when book designer Jane Gillespie and her husband, Ian, announced they would soon welcome a baby boy, it was only natural to throw a baby shower at the office.

Since Jane is there almost everyday and naturally very curious, it wasn't easy to keep it a surprise. In this case, most of the food was ordered from a nearby restaurant, with additional dishes added potluck-style to round out the selection.

Baby showers today have changed quite a bit. For one thing, they no longer just include women. The co-ed shower is the modern way to go. Admittedly, the women still do much of the cooking and planning, but the guys contribute in their own way.

Everyone in the office was asked to write a message for a baby quilt. Each message was then printed on swatches of fabric and sewn into a quilt by a co-worker. The result was touching and very personal.

» Computer generated letters were printed on paper and attached with diaper pins to hand towels. They were then clipped onto a clothes line.

## Invitations and Favors

The invitations were created on a computer using a traditional baby-blue palaka design then emailed to everyone in the office. RSVPs were taken by a designated coworker. The same palaka graphic was used to select the napkins, paper plates, and cups. Customized wrappings, which matched the invitations, covered store-purchased candy bars that were handed out as party favors.

We got Hapa!

Please join us for a

SURPRISE BABY SHOWER

# What to Pour

## pau hana punch

*To quench their thirst, the office staff opted for tubs of bottled water and pitchers of fruit punch. Try this refreshing drink at your next event.*

pineapple juice
pink grapefruit juice
ginger ale
pineapple spears and mint for garnish

1. Fill a punchbowl or individual pitchers half full of ice.

2. Pour in equal parts of pineapple juice, pink grapefruit juice, and ginger ale.

3. Stir and serve with more ice, pineapple spears, and sprigs of mint.

## Setting the Table

A conference room is ideal for an office party—setting up and keeping it a surprise is easier behind closed doors. Begin by covering the table with a standard white cloth. On top of that spread a top piece of blue palaka fabric.

For the centerpiece, fill a clear glass vase with fragrant plumeria from the backyard or use the Mom-To-Be's favorite flowers. Speaking of flowers, if you plan to give the expectant mother a lei, Island tradition dictates that it not be tied.

Hang a clothesline along one wall, and clip terrycloth towels and baby clothes with wooden clothespins and a message for the new parents. Along another wall, this office hung the handmade quilt. Round out the decorating by filling clear plastic baby bottles with bright orange jelly beans.

The food is served buffet-style on blue and white dishes.

# TIPS FOR A POTLUCK

- It's best to plan the menu. You may want to assign dishes, but be flexible. If someone is asked to make a vegetable dish and has a favorite in mind, let them do what they want. If you want specific dishes, distribute recipes.

- If you have non-cooks, suggest items that can be easily picked up at the grocery store such as a platter of crudités, paper products, or maki sushi.

- Most offices have a refrigerator and microwave. If possible, stay away from food that can't be served at room temperature or needs last-minute preparation.

- Pasta and chopped salads stand up well at potluck buffets, as do casseroles. Casseroles keep their warmth well, but if you are coming to the office in the morning, warming it up could be a problem. Take that into consideration when choosing a dish. Also, dress salads right before serving to prevent sogginess.

- Have someone pick up ice just prior to the party or bring it earlier and store in coolers.

- Designate a clean-up crew. Have plenty of plastic bags and aluminum foil for people to take home leftovers.

# TIMELINE

**Two weeks:** Create invitation on computer and e-mail to everyone in the office. Decide if you are going to give individual gifts or pool your money for one gift. Assign dishes if you are going to potluck.

**One week:** Using the computer, make name cards for the food, personalized covers for the candy bar favors. Purchase banner and decorations.

**Four days:** Order the cupcakes, sushi and chicken satay. Purchase paper goods.

**Two days:** Buy groceries for dish you will make.

**One day:** Buy fresh flowers.

**Morning of:** Pick up balloons if you plan to decorate with them. Arrange flowers. Set up the buffet and gift table.

**One to two hours:** Buy ice and bring a cooler. Food is delivered. Make the drinks.

**15 minutes:** Turn on music. Have everyone arrive early.

**Surprise!**

# menu

*hummus and corn chips*

*fresh hawaiian fruit salad*

*sweet pea salad*

*maki sushi*

*chicken satay*
*with peanut sauce*

*crudities with ranch dip*

*raisin breadsticks*

*individual vanilla lemon*
*cupcakes*

# Recipes

*Should you decide to try this party in a more intimate home setting,*
*or choose to bring something for potluck, here are the recipes.*

## chicken satay with peanut sauce

MAKES ABOUT 18 SKEWERS

6 chicken breasts, boneless and skinless
bamboo meat sticks (soak in water before using)

MARINADE:
1 tablespoon light brown sugar
2 tablespoons peanut butter
1/2 cup soy sauce
1/2 cup freshly squeezed lime juice
2 garlic cloves, minced
dried crushed chili pepper flakes to taste

1. Cut the chicken breasts into strips and thread onto the meat sticks.

2. In a bowl, mix together the marinade ingredients.

3. Place the meat skewers flat in a nonreactive baking dish or plastic zipped bag. Pour the marinade over the sticks.

4. Refrigerate overnight or for a minimum of 2 hours. Turn the sticks at least once in the marinade.

5. Remove the skewers from the refrigerator and bring to room temperature.

6. They can be broiled over charcoal or in the oven, turning once until cooked through.

7. Baste with the marinade while cooking then discard the sauce.

## PEANUT SAUCE:

2/3 cup crunchy peanut butter
1-1/2 cups coconut milk
1/4 cup freshly squeezed lemon juice
2 tablespoons soy sauce
2 tablespoons brown sugar
1 teaspoon fresh ginger, smashed

4 garlic cloves, minced
Cayenne pepper to taste
1/4 cup chicken broth
1/4 cup heavy cream
2 sprigs chopped fresh cilantro

8. In a saucepan over medium heat, cook the peanut butter, coconut milk, lemon juice, soy sauce, brown sugar, lime juice, garlic, and cayenne. Cook, stirring until the mixture thickens, about 15 minutes.

9. Remove from the stove and cool slightly.

10. Place the peanut mixture into a blender. Add the chicken broth and cream and blend until smooth. This can be made ahead of time and kept in the refrigerator until ready to serve.

11. Garnish with the chopped cilantro and serve on the side of the skewered meat.

## sweet pea salad

SERVES 6

one 10-ounce bag of frozen peas, thawed
1 cup celery, finely chopped
1/2 cup green onions, chopped
1 cup macadamia nuts or cashews, chopped

1/4 cup bacon, cooked crisp and crumbled
1 cup sour cream
1/2 teaspoon salt
1/4 cup Italian dressing

1. In a salad bowl, combine the peas, celery, green onions, nuts, and bacon.

2. In a small bowl, combine the sour cream, salt, and Italian dressing.

3. Pour the dressing over the pea mixture and mix lightly.

4. Refrigerate the salad about an hour to chill. Serve on lettuce leaves.

# HOLIDAY IN EDEN

# HOLIDAY IN EDEN

There is a certain something that happens when Karen and Leland Miyano are present. Their positive outlooks and their way of living life to the fullest brim over and sweep up everyone in their path. This is part of the reason an invitation to their legendary dinner parties is so coveted. It's not that the parties are so over-the-top fancy, but the magical combination of interesting people of all generations, their creative energy, and love of a good time makes you want to attend.

Leland is a sculptor and respected landscape designer who studied in Brazil. On the Windward side of O'ahu, large pieces of stone works-in-progress are scattered

about their dense tropical garden, which has been featured in many books and magazines. Karen is a talented caterer whose creations, while daunting to many, make her as gifted an artist as her husband. She is an advocate of using fresh, local ingredients and being environmentally conscious.

Several years ago, the couple began celebrating the feast of the Epiphany in early January. This date celebrates the arrival of the three wise men in Bethlehem and has long meant the end of the Christmas season.

## Invitations

Karen found the dictionary definition of "epiphany" and enlarged the wording for the invitations to accompany Leland's original artwork. To the party information, she added the guest list so that those coming could arrange to carpool.

If you're not one to create your own invitations, there are many stylish choices in stores during this time of year.

## What to Pour

Karen thinks nothing of making her own fresh ginger ale. Yet, there are many commercial drinks, such as pomegranate or cranberry juice, that mix well with lemon-lime soda for a tasty nonalcoholic drink. Make it more festive by running a lime around the rim of the glass and dipping it in a plate of colored holiday sugar available in specialty stores.

The sparkling Italian wine Prosecco looks wonderful served with a couple of fresh raspberries plopped into the glass.

Karen's pamplemousse cocktail is a pretty, rosy-hued holiday drink. Pamplemousse is just a fancier name for grapefruit.

# pamplemousse cocktail
### MAKES 6 DRINKS

7 tablespoons water
5 tablespoons pomegranate juice
1/4 cup sugar
4 teaspoons honey
18 fresh mint leaves, plus 6 sprigs for garnish
1-1/2 cups vodka
3/4 cup grapefruit juice
1/4 cup fresh lime juice

1. In a saucepan, bring the water, juice, sugar, and honey to a boil.

2. Stir to dissolve the sugar. Cool. This can be made the day before.

3. In a large pitcher, place the mint leaves and top with the mixture, vodka, grapefruit, and lime juice.

4. Fill with ice and stir vigorously.

5. Strain into martini glasses, garnish with a spring of mint and serve.

## Setting the Table

Because the Miyano's home is fairly small and their entertaining quotient big, they set up a pavilion-style dining area on their lānai. On it is a long table with chairs and places to put a buffet and bar. A remarkable chandelier, created by adding garden fairy lights and glass icicles to an old fixture, dominates the table.

The table is set with a botanical-patterned cloth, and variegated green branches from their garden are laid down the center of it. The plates are a simple white, and the glasses are green. Additional white tapers create another layer of light down the length of the table. Karen uses her collection of brass and ebony Thai flatware, which she picks up in secondhand stores and garage sales whenever she sees it.

The garden surrounding the lānai becomes an important part of the ambience. Strings of small garden lights are woven into the trees to create an enchanted, private Eden. Karen doesn't put up the traditional Christmas tree. Instead she strings lights on bare branches mounted on a stand and she and Leland hunt for fresh lump moss in the forest. Leland has created pieces of garden sculpture from tree bark and with that they mix found and secondhand items given to them by friends with good taste.

# TIMELINE

**Three weeks:** Create and mail invitations. Include a map if necessary.

**Two weeks:** Shop for candles, string lights and holiday tableware.

**One week:** Decorate the house. Buy new holiday music.

**5 days:** Buy liquor and wine for the bar.

**Three days:** Purchase groceries and flowers.

**Two days:** Set the table. Wash stemware and holiday dishes that may have been stored.

**One day:** Make the soup, marinate the flank steak, make the crêpes. Make or purchase the gingerbread. Prepare the pears.

**Day of:** Finish making the dinner. Make the vinaigrette and prepare the salad. Make the salmon dish and sauces.

**Two hours:** Ice the Prosecco. Mix the pamplemousse cocktails in a pitcher.

**One hour:** Grill the flank steak. Shower and dress.

**15 minutes:** Light the candles, turn on the music. Pour yourself a glass of wine.

**During the party:** Heat the soup. Assemble the crêpes and salmon dish. Toss the salad.

## Making It Easy

◆ So you don't live in a garden with a landscape designer husband? Hunt down fresh plants in garden shops and wholesale flower outlets. Home and garden catalogs are a great source of natural ornaments and tabletop items as well as outdoor lighting.

◆ Fill glass vases of all sizes with water and red food coloring. Float festive candles or add poinsettia flowers with sealed stems (use a match or lighter to burn the ends).

◆ If you're not a cook, hunt down good, frozen holiday pūpū. Heat it up, and you're ready to go. Order take-out dinners from your favorite restaurant and serve on pretty plates.

*Home and garden catalogs are a great source of natural ornaments and tabletop items as well as outdoor lighting.*

# THE HAWAIIAN WAY OF GIFTS

While Hawaiians give gifts for most of the same reasons anyone anywhere does, there are a few little rules of local etiquette to be aware of. For instance, whenever you are invited to someone's home you never go empty-handed. The gift need not be large or expensive. Something small from a recent trip, made in your kitchen, or the bounty of seasonal backyard produce are all acceptable. Many people take wine, preserves, or pretty hostess towels to simple home dinners.

This gift giving, likely adapted from Asian traditions, also includes events such as birthdays, graduations, weddings, childbirths, and funerals. Money, thought in some places to be crude and inappropriate, is always welcome at these events. The cash, check, or money order should always be placed in a personalized card. To simply hand someone the cash really is in poor taste. A good example of money-gifting is the presenting of money lei at such events as significant birthdays and graduations.

Lei are always acceptable. Try to match the flowers and size of the lei to the person receiving it. For example, women are often given smaller, fragrant lei such as pīkake, ginger and rose, while men often receive more "masculine" lei such as leaves strung with kukui, and cigar styles. Maile, either plain or entwined with ʻilima, pikake, pakalana, or mokihana, is often saved for very important occasions.

Omiyage, borrowed from the Japanese, is the tradition of giving money to those going on a trip and having them bring back a souvenir when they return. While this is not strictly observed today in the Islands, it is definitely good manners to return with something for your family and the office. Often it is something to eat such as cream puffs, manapua, boxes of candy, or cookies from the area you've been visiting.

# menu

*pamplemousse cocktails*

*homemade ginger ale prosecco*

*banana lemongrass and coconut
soup*

*flank steak in green tea crêpes
with plum wine sauce*

*salmon wrapped scallop with
mango chili lime, raspberry
chipotle puree, and jeweled
saffron basmati rice*

*asian pear arugula salad with
hazelnuts, shaved romano cheese,
and cumin vinaigrette*

*baked bittersweet chocolate
gingerbread with baked pears,
mascarpone crème, and edible
gold*

# Recipes

## banana lemongrass and coconut soup

SERVES 8–10

1/4 cup olive oil
1 cup very ripe sliced bananas
1-1/3 cup chopped onions
1 cup chopped leeks, white and pale green part
only (2 leeks)
1 cup chopped celery
3/4 cup chopped carrots
3 garlic cloves, chopped

1 tablespoon minced lemongrass, remove outer
stalks, use only bottom 2 inches
1/2 teaspoon hot chili paste (sambal oelek)
1/4 cup chopped fresh cilantro
1 teaspoon ground cumin
1 cup fresh orange juice
two 14-ounce cans vegetable broth
one 14-ounce can unsweetened coconut milk

1. Heat olive oil in a large saucepan over medium-high heat.

2. Sauté the bananas until they begin to brown, about 4 minutes.

3. Add the onion, leeks, celery, carrots, garlic, lemongrass, and chili paste. Sauté until the vegetables begin to brown, about 10 minutes.

4. Add the cilantro and cumin. Reduce heat and sauté another 2 minutes.

5. Add the orange juice and simmer for 2 minutes.

6. Add broth and simmer until the vegetables are tender, about 10 minutes.

7. Cool soup slightly.

8. Working in batches, purée the soup in a blender until smooth. Return the soup to the pan.

9. Add the coconut milk and simmer until warm, about 5 minutes.

10. Season with salt and pepper.

# flank steak in green tea crêpes with plum wine sauce

## FILLING FOR 2 DOZEN CRÊPES

1/2 cup plum wine
1/2 teaspoon kosher salt
1 teaspoon fresh grated ginger
2 garlic cloves, minced
3 tablespoons soy sauce
1/2 teaspoon chili paste
2 tablespoons fresh lime juice
1/4 cup honey
1-1/2 pounds flank steak

3 tablespoons prepared plum sauce
1/4 medium jicama, cut into 1/4-inch
matchsticks, about 2-1/2 inches long
1/2 red bell pepper, seeded and cut into
matchsticks, about 2-1/2 inches long
4 green onions, ends cut off and slivered into
long ties
Mint sprigs for garnish
1 recipe Green Tea Crêpes (see page 170)

1. In a bowl, combine the wine, salt, ginger, garlic, soy sauce, chili paste, lime juice, and honey, then stir.

2. Place the flank steak in a nonreactive dish and pour the wine marinade over it, turning to coat well.

3. Cover and marinate in the refrigerator for 6 hours or overnight.

4. Heat a grill or large grill pan.

5. Remove the steak from the marinade, place the steak on the grill and cook for 4-1/2 to 5 minutes. Turn and cook another 4 minutes for medium rare.

6. Transfer meat to a plate and cover with aluminum foil to cool slightly.

7. Place the reserved marinade in a saucepan and bring to a boil.

8. Reduce the marinade by half. Reduce the heat and whisk in the plum sauce.

9. Transfer sauce to a small serving bowl. Slice the steak across the grain into very thin slices.

# green tea crêpes

2 large eggs
1 cup milk
2 tablespoons unsalted butter, melted
1/2 teaspoon powdered green tea
1 cup flour
1/2 teaspoon sea salt
1/4 cup chopped green onion

1. In a large bowl, whisk the eggs, milk, 1/3 cup water and the butter.

2. Whisk in the green tea powder, flour, salt, and green onions, whisking until all the lumps have disappeared.

3. Transfer to an airtight container and refrigerate for at least thirty minutes or up to one day.

4. Heat a small nonstick crêpe pan or skillet over medium-low heat.

5. Stir batter if it has begun to separate.

6. Place 2 tablespoons of the batter into the warm skillet and swirl the pan to evenly coat the bottom. If it doesn't swirl easily, add 1 or 2 tablespoons of water to make the batter thinner.

7. Cook about 1 minute until the crêpe appears dry.

8. Gently flip the crêpe with a spatula and cook until it is lightly browned and slips easily in the pan, about 1 minute.

9. Transfer to a paper towel and cover with another towel, continuing until all the remaining batter is used. The crêpes may be made ahead and kept in the refrigerator, or frozen.

10. To assemble, place pieces of flank steak, jicama, and red pepper on the crêpe.

11. Drizzle with plum wine sauce.

12. Fold the bottom up, then the two sides, overlapping. Tie with a length of green onion. Garnish with sprig of mint.

# CHINATOWN NEW YEAR

# CHINATOWN NEW YEAR

Graphic designer David Cox and his friend Evelyn Kam, a production coordinator who spent much time shopping in Chinatown while growing up, still find inspiration in the annual preparations for Chinese New Year. The two decided to throw a party at the home of a friend.

They began on a Saturday morning with some very strong French coffee laced with sweet condensed milk at the Bale sandwich shop on King Street. Sufficiently wired, they began visiting their favorite stalls at the O'ahu Market, Kekaulike Market, and Maunakea Marketplace. A walk along Maunakea Street yielded small, dim sum-sized steamer baskets, dried lotus leaves, lucky bamboo, and New Year gao.

Once at home, the preparations began with recipes David created and has served to friends in the past. Evelyn set to work on the table. The stylish collaborative results can be seen here.

## Invitations

Being graphic designers, making invitations is both fun and easy for David and Evelyn. However, we suggest you look through Chinese shops for seasonal cards, red li see envelopes, and other such paper items. Red and gold are this holiday's special colors. Red brings energy and good luck. Gold brings good fortune, of course.

# TIMELINE

**Three weeks:**
Mail your invitations.

**One week:** Select your menu and make your shopping list. Call ahead if you are planning to order your food from a Chinese restaurant.

**Three days:** Raid your own closets for linens, decorative items and anything red. Clean your house.

**Two days:** Shop for groceries. Order dessert if you aren't going to make it. Visit a wine shop with your menu in hand. Make sure you have plastic trash bags.

**One day:** Purchase any fresh seafood. Set your table. Select music and put in your CD player. Set up your bar.

**Morning of:** Prep your food for last-minute cooking. Make any sauces or condiments. Pull out the pots and pans you will need. Bring out your serving dishes. Print a copy of your menu to have in your kitchen as you prepare.

**Five hours:** Purchase ice and place into a cooler. Empty your dishwasher. Check that your bathroom is presentable and has guest towels and nice soap.

**Two hours:** Chill your white wines. Send someone to pickup the food if ordered from a restaurant.

**One hour:** Turn on the music. Make yourself a dressing drink. Take a shower.

**During party:** Steam the seafood items prior to serving.

# What to Pour

## lychee martini
### MAKES 1 DRINK

2 ounces good quality vodka
1 teaspoon syrup from can of lychees
1 rambutan for garnish
(found seasonally in Chinatown markets)

1. Place the vodka in a shaker with lots of ice.

2. Add 1 teaspoon of the syrup from a can of lychees. Reserve the lychees for garnish if you cannot find rambutan, or for a fruit salad or dessert.

3. Shake well and strain into a martini glass.

4. Slice the pod of a rambutan and attach to the rim of the glass for garnish. *Rambutan are round, red, and prickly-looking. The peeled fruit looks much like a lychee, but the taste is somewhat different.*

### ✦ ✦ ✦ N O T E ✦ ✦ ✦

For a sweeter martini use 1 teaspoon of lychee syrup in place of the syrup from the can, or add 1 teaspoon of triple sec to the recipe above.

# WELCOMING THE LUNAR YEAR

Chinese New Year is celebrated on the first day of the first month of the lunar year. This comes during the end of January or early February and is marked by the Chinese and Vietnamese communities in Hawai'i. Laotians celebrate closer to the Buddhist New Year in April.

This is a time to clean your house, pay all your debts, honor your ancestors, see your family, and eat good food. The traditional holiday foods are long beans and noodles signifying long life; citrus fruits such as oranges, tangerines and pomelo; and sweets like candied coconut, carrots, water chestnuts, and lotus root. Throughout Chinatown you will find gao, which is made with sweet, glutinous rice flour, wrapped with red paper, and topped with a sprinkling of sesame seeds. The roundness of the gao represents the unity of the family, and the sesame seeds are a wish for many children.

In Honolulu's Chinatown, a dragon, symbolizing good luck and virility, usually leads a parade. Firecrackers are set off, according to an old folk tale, to ward off evil. The bad spirits don't like the loud noise. It is also a time for telling fortunes and playing games of chance such as mah jong and payute.

Evelyn sets the table with vintage Rose Medallion Canton ware and golden chargers.

## Setting the Table

Both David and Evelyn believe in using what you already have, but rethinking it. They found a rich, but quietly brocaded tablecloth that had been purchased inexpensively from Ross for Less. In the pantry they discovered a black and red lacquered container used for serving rice. This, piled with a fresh cluster of prickly, red rambutan became the centerpiece. To that they added Asian objects found around the house and stuffed into closets. Dig around in your own closets. Traditional ware doesn't have to be the only thing that ends up on your table.

They used collectible old Canton dishes in a rose medallion pattern from their friend's grandmother to set the table. Under the plates they put gold chargers to liven up the look. Vintage red glassware, also found in the closet, completed the setting. The lesson here is to look for complementary colors and designs in the spirit and mood you want to create. You may already own much of it.

## Making It Easy

+ Set the table with a crisp white linen cloth and white dishes. Look for inexpensive colorful rice bowls and chopsticks in a bargain store like Marukai. Buy flowering narcissus plants and cluster them in the center. Use red pillar candles. Place red and gold Chinese good luck papers at each place setting.

+ Order out for food from your favorite Chinese restaurant (remember that Vietnamese also celebrate the same holiday) and serve family-style at the table. Rieslings are nice with Asian food.

## menu

*steamed lotus leaf prawns with*
*black bean sauce*

*black coconut rice*

*long beans with*
*szechuan honey glaze*

*steamed sea bass on ocean salad*
*with tobiko butter sauce*

# Recipes

## steamed sea bass
## on ocean salad with
## tobiko butter sauce

SERVES 4

1 pound ocean salad (found in the fish section of local supermarkets)
2 pounds boneless, skinned, firm sea bass cut into four fillets
1 cup good sake
4 tablespoons unsalted butter
3 tablespoons mirin (sweet Japanese cooking wine)
1 small package tobiko
black sesame seeds for garnish

1. Place a bamboo steamer over a wok with 2 cups of water for steaming.

2. Line the bottom of the steamer with the ocean salad. Retain 1 cup of the salad for garnish.

3. Place the sea bass on top of the ocean salad in the steamer. Pour the sake over the sea bass and place a lid on the steamer.

4. Steam the fish for 12 to 15 minutes, until fish shows no sign of translucency.

5. In a saucepan, add the butter and mirin.

6. When butter has melted and is well mixed with the mirin, remove from heat and stir in 1 heaping tablespoon of the tobiko.

7. On a serving platter arrange four small mounds of the remaining ocean salad.

8. Place on each a sea bass filet. Over each piece of sea bass ladle the butter mixture.

9. Place a teaspoon of tobiko on each fillet and garnish with a small sprinkle of toasted black sesame seeds.

# steamed lotus leaf prawns with black bean sauce

## SERVES 4

8 large prawns, remove shells but leave the tail on
4 dried lotus leaves (may be found in Chinatown markets)
2 tablespoons black bean sauce
2 tablespoons mirin (sweet Japanese cooking wine)
1 green onion, chopped for garnish

1. Remove shells from prawns leaving the tail intact.

2. Butterfly by slicing through the back of the prawn where the vein is. Remove the vein and place the prawns on a plate so they lay flat.

3. Place the dried lotus leaves under warm water briefly to soften.

4. Take four small bamboo steamers (dim sum size) and line with the lotus leaves.

5. Place two prawns in each steamer on top of the lotus leaf and place lids on the steamers.

6. Place the steamer baskets on a rack over a pot of boiling water and steam for 6 to 10 minutes until the prawns are pink.

7. Place 2 tablespoons of black bean sauce in a bowl. Add 2 tablespoons of mirin and 1 tablespoon of water. Mix well.

8. Remove bamboo steamers from rack and remove the lids.

9. Place 4 baskets on a serving tray, drizzle the prawns with the black bean sauce, and garnish with green onions.

# black coconut rice

### SERVES 4

3 cups coconut milk
1-1/2 cups black rice (may be found in Chinatown markets)

1. In a saucepan, bring the coconut milk to a slow boil. Stir in black rice.

2. Turn heat down to simmer and place a lid on the pan.

3. Place a damp towel over the top of the lid.

4. Simmer for about 30 minutes, or until all the liquid is absorbed. Gently stir the rice with a fork.

5. Serve in rice bowls.

# long beans with szechuan honey glaze

## SERVES 4

1 pound Chinese long beans (may be found in markets in Chinatown) or green beans
4 tablespoons unsalted butter
2 tablespoons dark, thick soy sauce
2 tablespoons honey
1/2 teaspoon red pepper flakes
thinly sliced orange peel for garnish

1. Wash and place the green beans in a steamer basket.

2. Steam for 10 to 12 minutes until tender.

3. Place the butter in a small saucepan and melt over medium heat. Add the soy sauce, honey, and red pepper flakes.

4. Bring mixture to a slow bubble. Remove from heat.

5. Place green beans in a serving dish.

6. Drizzle the sauce over the beans and garnish with thin slices of orange peel.

# APPENDIX

## NAME THE OCCASION

Fat Tuesday, Lei Day, baby lūʻau, sunset weddings on the beach, beach park BBQs with family, dim sum with friends, Super Bowl parties, wedding showers, birthdays—there are endless reasons to get together and celebrate, or no reason at all, other than a festive mood and a tasty new recipe you'd like to share.

## THINK ABOUT YOUR OPTIONS

Once you know what you're celebrating, it's time to brainstorm ideas and map out a plan. Some factors to consider are these:

- How many people do you want or need to invite? Can you fit them into your apartment or house, or do you need to take your party elsewhere?

- Do you enjoy cooking and want to highlight your skills, even if they're in the developing stage? Or perhaps you would like to cook one or two dishes and pick up the rest from a deli?

- Maybe you would prefer to have someone else do ALL your cooking for you. There are endless options—take-out menus, party trays, caterers, a posh restaurant downtown, or your favorite hole-in-the-wall—anything can work.

- What's your budget? Can you afford to supply all the food and drinks, or would you prefer that your guests bring potluck or split the restaurant bill? Can they afford it?

- Do you need help with your party, such as full-service caterer, a neighbor's teenager to serve and clean up, a friend to mix drinks, or a relative to bring ice and help with parking? If more than fifteen to twenty people are coming to your home, definitely plan on getting help!

- What time will you throw your party? Is this a group of adults who like to stay up late, or a multigenerational affair where the youngest and oldest guests have early bedtimes and inflexible naptimes?

- Will you serve alcohol? If so, do you need a well-stocked bar, or will wine and beer suffice? Perhaps you can add a single theme-based cocktail to the selection? Or maybe your party will work best without any alcohol.

## PREPARE YOUR LISTS

Once you have all the details down, the key to a successful, enjoyable party is planning. Make lists of your menu, grocery items, invitees, timelines, decorations and favors, things to borrow, shops to visit, what to bring, etc. The more you organize and prepare in advance, the more you'll actually enjoy your party. Look at the menus, timelines, and sidebars in these pages for guidance, or read on for more tips and ideas.

## SETTLE ON A SETTING

If your party exceeds the capacity of your apartment or home, move the event off-site. Some possibilities:

- Co-host a party with a friend or relative with more space, either inside or out. Carports, lānai, and lawns can make great settings.

- Reserve a room at a favorite restaurant, from an oceanfront hotel in Waikīkī to historic locales like the Queen Emma Summer Palace to your favorite undiscovered gem in Chinatown.

- Take your party to the park. Magic Island and Kapiʻolani parks beckon in town, while beautiful beach parks line the islands. For events exceeding fifty people, you'll need to get a permit. Call the Parks Permit Office at 523-4527 or go to **www.honolulu.gov/parks/parkuse/html** for more information.

- Search for smaller, hidden parks, such as the Waʻahila Ridge State Recreation Area in a forest high above Honolulu or the weekend party hall at Heʻeia State Park, with gorgeous, sweeping views of Kāneʻohe Bay.

- Go camping. It's a far cry from an elegant dinner party for six, but it sure is fun to roast hot dogs and marshmallows by a fire, especially if kids are involved. See **www.hawaii.gov/dlnr/dsp/index.html** for information on state parks, including camping permits and fees.

- Charter a boat or a trolley for a sunset cruise through the waters or streets of Waikīkī.

- Build an underground imu and slow-cook a Thanksgiving turkey or an Easter pig.

- Rent the Waikīkī Aquarium for a big, unforgettable sunset bash.

• Bring the kids for some birthday fun at the Honolulu Zoo, Great Adventures Water Park, the Ice Palace, box car racing in Kunia, bounce houses, and more.

• Reassess your own apartment, and think about how it might work, no matter how small. Lower your headcount. Borrow side tables for a buffet. Modify a sit-down dinner to a mix-and-mingle cocktail party. Your guests will love the warmth and intimacy of being invited into your home to share a meal or a special occasion.

## DECIDE WHAT TO SERVE AND POUR

• Use the recipes featured in these pages for elegant, delicious fare that is sure to impress, or wow your guest with your own favorite recipes.

• Reduce the stress by making just one or two dishes and buying the rest.

• Have someone else handle ALL the food. Caterers, take-out menus, private dining rooms, potluck in the park—the options are endless.

• Let your theme or setting dictate your food choices. A BBQ is natural for backyard or park celebrations, while Chinese New Year or a welcome-home-from-Tuscany party call for international flavors.

• Simplify your pūpū. A nice cheese, an assortment of crackers, and a bowl of salty nuts will work just fine, as will some store-bought dim sum, poke, and sashimi or hummus, salsa, and chips.

• Purchase ready-to-go salads and toss with high-quality bottled dressing.

• Shop a local Farmer's Market for the freshest fruits, vegetables, coffee, condiments, baked goods, and more. The Saturday morning market at Kapiʻolani Community College has some choice selections. To find a market near you, go to **www.hawaii.gov/hdoa/add/farmers-market-in-hawaii/**.

• Cut corners with dessert. Decorate a store-bought cake with fresh flowers or a frozen pound cake with fresh berries and whipped cream. And don't be embarrassed to use cake mixes and prepared crusts—they're good!

• Dress up prepared foods with fresh garnishes, such as lemons for lemon chicken or basil leaves for pasta with pesto. Ti leaves are beautiful on serving trays.

• Tailor your menu to match your serving style. If your guests will be balancing plates on their laps, don't serve them messy sauces or food that requires a knife.

- Get rid of flimsy aluminum trays. Take-out food looks better and even tastes better on attractive serving platters.

- Remember that buffets are the easiest way to serve, but they require greater quantities of food than a sit-down dinner, where you can exert some portion control.

- Stock your bar (or your cooler) like a pro.

## PREPARE YOUR PROVISIONS

- Picture the event in your head and map out what you will need: folding tables and chairs; tents and umbrellas; lawn mats; coolers and lots and lots of ice; plates, cups, utensils; serving spoons and a cake knife; table clothes and napkins; sunscreen and bug spray; flowers and candles; paper towels and garbage bags; charcoal, lighter fluid, and matches; a CD player or karaoke machine...you get the idea.

- Take inventory of what you already have lurking in cabinets, closets, and drawers. If it's a dinner party, make sure you have enough tableware to accommodate your guests, and don't be afraid to mix and match or supplement with items from discount stores.

- Visit the restaurant or party venue, if that's your route. Figure out what they can provide in the way of décor, and whether you want to embellish the setting (with tablecloth toppers, votive candles, or flowers, for example).

- Borrow, buy, or rent what you don't have. Wholesale clubs, as well as discount and secondhand stores, are great for both long-term investments and throw-away items. Look for rental bargains too, such as the Leisure Center (**www.hawaii.edu/cclp**), which rents jumbo coolers and other outdoor gear for just a few dollars to students and staff at the University of Hawai'i at Mānoa.

- Store your provisions in a single spot for quick, ready access on party day.

## GET THE WORD OUT

Your main goal is to get information to your guests, including the date, time, and place of the event. Be sure to include your phone number or email address for RSVPs, as well as parking instructions and any dress requests. Include maps if necessary (**www.mapquest.com**). And be clear about what food will be served. If your guest list includes kids, vegetarians, or anyone with food allergies, you'll need to let them know what's on the menu and offer suitable choices, if possible.

Deliver your invitations using any method that works for you. Phone calls, email, or free online services (**www.evite.com**) are all functional and fine. But if you have some time and are willing to put in a little effort, traditional invitations delivered via the post office add a nice touch. Invitations should be in the mail at least two weeks prior to the event, a month in advance for a fancy occasion or holiday party.

You don't have to be an artist to make your invitation stand out. Here are a few ideas:
- Purchase blank stationery and personalize with colored paper, decorative flowers, stamps, buttons, ribbon, or anything you'd like. Write the party details by hand, and insert in a brightly colored envelope.
- Maintain your theme by downloading or scanning party-related images, then printing them directly onto card stock.
- Pull out the construction paper, rubber stamps, stickers, markers, and more and let your kids—or even the whole neighborhood gang—create original masterpieces.
- Buy logo cards or gift shop items from the restaurant, hotel, or venue where your party will take place.
- Use the theme or color of your invitations on your paper goods and decorations for a unified look.

## MAKE IT FESTIVE AND MEMORABLE
- Get creative and pick a theme—any theme will work! A "pink party" in honor of Girls' Day, a Bollywood birthday to celebrate Indian style, or a Liliko'i Festival to take advantage of a lush vine full of ripened fruit.
- Let your theme and setting determine your décor—the good luck color red at Chinese New Year or a Yakudoshi party, luminarias lining your entryway for Cinco de Mayo, balloons and plastic bugs for the young naturalist's birthday.
- Consider lei and party favors, which are always a hit in Hawai'i. Again, let your theme lead you to ideas, and keep your eyes open for interesting shops and great bargains.
- Choose games to play if they tie in to your party (i.e. an egg hunt for Easter).
- Decorate your table, even if you're budget-conscious and style-challenged. Cluster pillar-style candles on a tray surrounded by pebbles or sand, or buy some supermarket flowers, trim the stems low, and place them in glasses.

- Think beyond candles and flowers. Anything that works with your theme or colors can look good on your table. If you're at the beach, jars filled with candles and coral can serve as excellent table décor.

- Choose linen and cotton over synthetic tablecloths, if at all possible.

- Clear the clutter to make space for food, pūpū, and drinks. Stash away magazines, knick-knacks, and fragile items.

- Remove personal items from bathroom counters, and put out fresh flowers and hand towels.

- Make sure everything is clean, but don't obsess on spotlessness.

- Turn on the outdoor lights or lanterns when the sun sets, or dim the lights and turn up the music if you're indoors.

- Enjoy your party!

# ACKNOWLEDGMENTS

There are so many people whose guidance, friendship and vigorous good taste went into the making of this book. Foremost among them are all the talented people whose parties are at the heart of this endeavor. They are: Jeff and Marion Philpotts Miller and their children Makena and Maree, Larry Heim, Amerjit Ghag and their children Indigo and Arjuna, Stacie Hurtado, Carrie Nakano and Amy Lee, Jonathan Staub and Jeff Finney, Gerri Miyamoto, Shanlyn Park, Joelle Kane, Lia Dwight, Trish Morikawa; Keli Hustace and Emiko Fujiwara of Natsunoya Teahouse, Gay Wong, Karen and Leland Miyano, David Cox and Evelyn Kam.

The gang at Mutual Publishing, Angie Britten, Nicole Sakai and production director Jane Gillespie have been so supportive of this project and I thank them. Graphic designer Julie Chun worked so hard to give the book its fresh, contemporary look.

Then there's Kaz Tanabe who works so fast you don't realize what he's shot. He has such a wonderful way of seeing things you never knew were there. Now here is a quietly adventurous spirit. David Franzen made beautiful photographs for the Bollywood Birthday, Girl's Day and Teahouse parties. He's always a pleasure to work with.

How can I not thank Mary Philpotts McGrath for her continuing friendship and generosity. She so generously opened her home for photographs and is always a source of ideas and information.

I neglected in the past to thank my good friend, Lynne Horner, for her wonderful, artful styling of food photographs and would like to recognize her here.

Then there are those who let me talk their ears off – Marion, Jon, Woozer and Dougie. How can I forget Betty Fullard Leo, Rita Ariyoshi, Cheryl Tsutsumi, Lloyd Jones, Marcie and Rick Carroll for lots of laughs and good advice. Joan Namkoong is a continuing source of inspiration.

If I've forgotten anyone, please forgive me.


Kaui Philpotts